"God is calling His church [...] This book is evidence of w[...] [...] part of what He is doing. W[...] [...] about Debbie's book is the variety. She helps us understand a number of different types of prayer and several different spiritual disciplines linked to prayer. You will find knowledge, know-how, how-to, insights, models, and guidelines in this book and be stimulated and encouraged to continue in the ministry of prayer."

—BENNIE MOSTERT, director, Jericho Walls International; international coordinator, International Prayer Council

"The messages that are on Debbie's heart are urgently needed among us in these desperate days in which we live. I see a great increase of emphasis on praise and worship, especially when there is great music, but I see very little time being given to intercessory prayer. I believe this book will help people move in the right direction in learning how to pray."

—GEORGE VERWER, founder and former international director, Operation Mobilization

"Debbie Przybylski's insights on prayer are hard-won. They come from years and years spent in the presence of God and with other intercessors. As Debbie's pastor, I have been a firsthand witness to her own prayer life and remarkable gift of faith. I heartily commend her writings, as they are written by a practitioner, not a theorist. Debbie is the real thing, and it comes through every sentence she writes."

—NATE ATWOOD, senior pastor, Kempsville Presbyterian Church, Virginia Beach, Virginia

"The teaching contained in this book is first from the position of intimacy, listening to the Father's heart, and then from experience gained from ministry in many difficult countries, many with Operation Mobilization. It is about changing the destiny of nations through prayer. There is a river of prayer that is sweeping the globe—prayer out of hunger, desperation, and weakness, but also out of sheer abandonment to a God who passionately loves His children and wants our hearts undivided. Debbie's writings have challenged me to dive into this river and join in what God is doing. As you read, allow the Holy Spirit to whisper to you to live and pray as though nothing is impossible."

—GRAHAM WELLS, Global Prayer Ministries, Operation Mobilization USA, former director, O.M. Ship Logos

Personal Prayer That
Changes the World

INTERCESSORS
ARISE

Debbie Przybylski

OUR GUARANTEE TO YOU

For a free catalog
of NavPress books & Bible studies call
1-800-366-7788 (USA) or 1-800-839-4769 (Canada).

www.NavPress.com

The Navigators is an international Christian organization. Our mission is to advance the gospel of Jesus and His kingdom into the nations through spiritual generations of laborers living and discipling among the lost. We see a vital movement of the gospel, fueled by prevailing prayer, flowing freely through relational networks and out into the nations where workers for the kingdom are next door to everywhere.

NavPress is the publishing ministry of The Navigators. The mission of NavPress is to reach, disciple, and equip people to know Christ and make Him known by publishing life-related materials that are biblically rooted and culturally relevant. Our vision is to stimulate spiritual transformation through every product we publish.

© 2008 by Debbie Przybylski

All rights reserved. No part of this publication may be reproduced in any form without written permission from NavPress, P.O. Box 35001, Colorado Springs, CO 80935. www.navpress.com

NAVPRESS and the NAVPRESS logo are registered trademarks of NavPress. Absence of ® in connection with marks of NavPress or other parties does not indicate an absence of registration of those marks.

Visit *PRAY!* at www.praymag.com

ISBN-13: 978-1-60006-223-0
ISBN-10: 1-60006-223-7

Cover design by The DesignWorks Group, David Uttley, www.thedesignworksgroup.com
Cover image by Shutterstock
Creative Team: Dave Wilson, Susan Martins Miller, Cara Iverson, Lora Schrock, Darla Hightower, Arvid Wallen, Kathy Guist

Some of the anecdotal illustrations in this book are true to life and are included with the permission of the persons involved. All other illustrations are composites of real situations, and any resemblance to people living or dead is coincidental.

Unless otherwise specified, Scripture quotations in this publication are taken from the HOLY BIBLE: NEW INTERNATIONAL VERSION® (NIV®). Copyright © 1973, 1978, 1984 by International Bible Society. Used by permission of Zondervan Publishing House. All rights reserved. Other versions used include: the *New American Standard Bible* (NASB), © The Lockman Foundation 1960, 1962, 1963, 1968, 1971, 1972, 1973, 1975, 1977, 1995.

Library of Congress Cataloging-in-Publication Data

Przybylski, Debbie, 1953-
  Intercessors arise : personal prayer that changes the world / Debbie
Przybylski.
    p. cm.
  Includes bibliographical references.
  ISBN 978-1-60006-223-0
  1. Intercessory prayer--Christianity. I. Title.
BV215.P79 2008
248.3'2--dc22

2007036992

Printed in the United States of America

1 2 3 4 5 6 7 8 / 12 11 10 09 08

To my husband, Norman, my partner in life and in ministry.
Thank you for your heart for people and your sacrificial love for
the nations. Your heart has greatly impacted and inspired my life.

CONTENTS

Foreword by Eddie Smith   9

Acknowledgments   11

Introduction   13

Chapter One: The Intercessor and Intimacy   17
    Practicing His Presence: Becoming a Best Friend of God
    A Sustained Pursuit After God's Own Heart
    Longings of the Heart

Chapter Two: The Intercessor and Faith   31
    Faith-Filled Prayers Developed Through Delay
    Prayers of Faith for the Impossible
    Dependence—God's Unlimited Opportunity to Bless

Chapter Three: The Intercessor and Character   47
    A Humble Heart
    Words That Uplift and Bring Grace
    Joyful in Prayer

Chapter Four: The Intercessor and Stillness   67
    Maximum Effectiveness Through Waiting on God
    Listening to God—Hearing His Voice
    Soaking in God's Presence

Chapter Five: The Intercessor and the Bible   81
    Praying the Bible

Praying God's Promises
Meditation and Prayer

Chapter Six: The Intercessor and Persistence   97
Persistent Prayer
Burden-Bearing Intercession
The Diligence of Prayer

Chapter Seven: The Intercessor and Purpose   115
Purpose-Driven Prayer
A Call to Focused Living
Prayer Discovers God's Agenda

Chapter Eight: The Intercessor and Strongholds   131
Destroying Personal Strongholds
God Is My Stronghold
Choose Life

Chapter Nine: The Intercessor and Forgiveness   149
The Power of Forgiveness
The Choice of Forgiveness
The Freedom of Forgiveness

Chapter Ten: The Intercessor and Revival   165
The Human Characteristics of Revival
The Supernatural Fire of Revival
Preparation for Revival

Chapter Eleven: The Intercessor and the World   179
Bringing the Touch of Jesus Through Prayer
Looking into the Heart of God for the Nations
The Salt of the Earth and the Light of the World

Conclusion   199

Notes   201

Recommended Reading   205

About the Author   209

About Intercessors Arise International   211

FOREWORD

TODAY I RECEIVED an e-mail from a dear intercessor in another city. She said, "Please tell me how your wife, Alice, can mentor me in intercession." I had to tell her that Alice travels around the world equipping Christian leaders and can't possibly mentor individual intercessors any longer. When we were local pastors, we loved that part of ministry, but that was more than a dozen years ago!

I understand this woman's desire to have a guide. I've also heard Alice lament that she never had a mentor. She had to learn intercession the old-fashioned way: She had to earn it. She would have dearly loved to have an experienced person show her the way.

Have you ever felt that way? If so, then I have good news for you—meet your mentor!

Our friend Debbie Przybylski knows the way. Not only that, she also has one of the finest gifts of written teaching I've seen anywhere. And this book is a perfect example of it. In *Intercessors Arise* she addresses intercession and its relationship to worship, passion, faith, character, stillness, the Word, intimacy with God, and much more.

Intercessors Arise will strengthen your personal prayer life. It is also excellent for developing group prayer. Each chapter contains three separate teachings that will assist your spiritual growth and motivation in prayer. The teachings are designed for reading again and again according to your particular need of the moment, and for prayerful consideration and application.

Eddie Smith
author of *How to Be Heard in Heaven*;
president, U.S. Prayer Center

ACKNOWLEDGMENTS

WITH SPECIAL THANKS:

To the Holy Spirit, who gave me the privilege to partner with You in writing this book. I was always aware of Your strength and supernatural help in every topic pertaining to prayer and intercession. I learned so much about Your heart for intercession, and I am so blessed in being part of what You are doing all throughout the world in prayer.

To my husband, Norman, who encouraged me and gave me freedom to pursue this ministry of Intercessors Arise. Thank you for releasing me to focus on intercession.

To Susan Martins Miller, Jeanne Allen, and Debbie Leseberg, who gave many hours of hard work in editing this book. I am so grateful for your perseverance, insight, and expertise.

To the Elijah Company, Inc., board of directors, who encouraged us in the ministry of Elijah Company, Inc., and Intercessors Arise. Thank you for listening, advising, praying, and encouraging us in this ministry. You believed in us even during the hard times. Thank you for your rock-solid faith.

To all the intercessors who have faithfully prayed for us.

Without your encouragement and prayers, this would not have been possible. I value your prayers more than you could ever know.

INTRODUCTION

Prayer is not an indifferent or a small thing. It is not a sweet, little privilege. It is a great prerogative, far-reaching in its effects. Failure to pray entails losses far beyond the person who neglects it. Prayer is not a mere episode of the Christian life. Rather, the whole of life is a preparation for and the result of prayer.
E. M. Bounds, *E. M. Bounds on Prayer*[1]

THE MINISTRY OF Intercessors Arise was birthed in my heart years ago on the mission field as a young missionary trying to reach the world with the gospel of Jesus Christ. It was then that I saw the desperate need for prayer for the nations. Over the years, my passion for intercession grew. Praying in the nations over many years with Operation Mobilization on its mission ship *Doulos* and ministering in more than sixty countries was a privilege. I saw prayer as a vital necessity in reaching the world. I learned the blessing of both personal and corporate prayer for the lost. Intercessors Arise began the week after 9/11.

Throughout the years, I have had the honor of being involved in prayer with people from all over the world and from all denominations, backgrounds, and ages. Perhaps this is why I believe so strongly in God's creative diversity in prayer and in His many ways of expressing Himself through His people. It has been a delight and joy to participate in so many prayer meetings in various nations on every continent.

During the past few years, my passion for prayer has grown into an earnest desire to see intercession increase and develop throughout the world. The prayer movement is spreading rapidly and growing with intensity. Countries everywhere are being touched with the power of prayer. My desire is to help train and motivate you for this worldwide prayer movement. I want to offer preparation in personal prayer that will change the world.

To help attain this goal, I wrote *Intercessors Arise*, a mentoring manual for prayer and intercession in the end times. Designed to cross all denominational and cultural barriers, it is written both for individuals who are learning to pray and for those who are well-seasoned intercessors.

Some people have said to me, "I don't have the gift of intercession," and then have grown to be mighty prayer warriors. None of us is born a prayer hero. We become one through practice. Intercessory prayer is an extension of the ministry of Jesus through His church on earth. He works through the prayers of His people. Through intercession, we mediate between God and humans as His representatives on earth, standing between Him and a lost world.

God is calling the entire body of Christ to pray and to intercede. Jesus is our example as the greatest intercessor, and He invites us to join Him. This is both our responsibility and a wonderful privilege to partner with God as we pray. We bring people to God in prayer, asking Him to meet with them. With His authority, we enforce the victory of Calvary here on earth through our prayers. Now we must awaken to this glorious privilege.

Intercessors Arise can be used for strengthening the individual prayer life and developing group praying. Each chapter has three separate teachings that are short and practical with the hope of launching you further than you have ever been in the tremendous ministry of world-changing prayer. Each chapter ends with a personal application assignment designed for individuals as well as for training in groups. My desire is that you not only learn and grow in intercession but also begin to train others. Each chapter ends with an application prayer.

If you want to grow in your personal prayer life and make an impact in your world through intercession, then this book is for you. God is calling each one of us to rise higher in prayer than ever before. It's time for us to meet this challenge. It's time to release God on earth through our prayers. I encourage you as you read this book to make a new commitment to steadfast, earnest prayer.

My intense hope is to see intercessors arise in the end times. The days are getting darker, the need is getting greater, and the expectation of a worldwide harvest is growing brighter. I pray that you arise to the call for prayer and intercession in your own life, whether it is for your family, your city, your nation, or the world. It is time for expansion and increase on a global scale. It is time for fervency of intercession to develop beyond anything we have ever seen or imagined. May you arise in intercession for such a time as this. May you arise in personal prayer that changes the world.

> *Arise, shine, for your light has come,*
> *and the glory of the LORD rises upon you.*

See, darkness covers the earth
     and thick darkness is over the peoples,
but the LORD rises upon you
     and his glory appears over you. (Isaiah 60:1-2)

CHAPTER ONE

THE INTERCESSOR AND INTIMACY

Love the Lord your God with all your heart and with all your soul and with all your mind and with all your strength.

— Mark 12:30

WE ALL SAT on the edge of our seats, nearly breathless. Standing before us was Corrie ten Boom, who had been sent to a concentration camp because her family protected Jewish refugees from Nazi persecution. It was my first year in Bible school, and Corrie had come to speak for our chapel service. She told about her difficult days surviving in that camp and how God sustained her day by day. At the time, I didn't know much about her, but I was immediately aware of the abiding presence of God in her life. Something was different—radiant—about her countenance as she shared how she was able to see God's grace and glory in the deepest darkness because she was so intimately acquainted with Him. She knew the price of intimacy as she spent her days in intercession in that lice-infested prison. Corrie practiced God's presence in even the gloomiest, darkest situation. She pursued His heart at a time when there was no apparent hope of escape or deliverance. Even in such a horrific place, the grace and majesty of God permeated the heart of Corrie ten Boom.

Her message was clear: Intimacy with God will help us to live victoriously in even the most difficult circumstances. But the challenge was also clear: How do we grow in intimacy with Him?

Let's explore some ways we can practice God's presence and pursue God's heart. We'll see how God can meet the longings of our hearts and awaken us to a fascinating life of intimacy.

PRACTICING HIS PRESENCE: BECOMING A BEST FRIEND OF GOD

Knowing and loving God is our greatest privilege, and being known and loved is God's greatest pleasure.

— Rick Warren, *The Purpose-Driven Life*

What a privilege to become a best friend of God! Have you grasped the reality of what this means?

As a humble cook in a seventeenth-century French monastery, Brother Lawrence was able to turn even a boring job, such as washing dishes, into an act of worship and an opportunity to build his relationship with God. He said, "The key to friendship with God is not changing what you do, but changing your attitude toward what you do. What you normally do for yourself you begin doing for God, whether it is eating, bathing, working, relaxing, or taking out the trash."[1] We read in Psalm 16:11,

You have made known to me the path of life;
  you will fill me with joy in your presence,
  with eternal pleasures at your right hand.

Following Brother Lawrence's example, let's realize that worship should not be so much an event as a perpetual attitude.

I once read about a man who said that he wanted to learn to pray all the time in every situation day and night. He wanted to live in constant fellowship with God and moment-by-moment companionship with Jesus. This is a holy ambition and motivates me personally to develop this kind of intimate relationship with God. When we pray, we are speaking to God, and when we meditate on God's Word, He speaks to us. We need both as we develop our friendship with God. Practicing the presence of God will give us rest and lead us into a more fruitful lifestyle. But how can we practice God's presence on a daily basis?

Use Breath Prayers. Pray a brief phrase to Jesus throughout the day that you can repeat in one breath. You may want to pray phrases such as, "You will help me," "You promise to never leave me," "I can do all things through Christ," "Your joy is my strength," "I love You," and "Help me trust You." Breath prayers, unlike regular prayers, are short with just a few words that you can quickly pray to God at any time. They will keep you more conscious of your relationship with God on a moment-by-moment basis. You become more aware that He is with you through all the joys and sorrows of daily life. You realize in a deeper dimension His companionship. As time goes on, it becomes a natural practice in your everyday life, and you realize afresh that Jesus really is your best friend. The promise of Exodus 33:14 becomes more real: "My Presence will go with you, and I will give you rest." A deeper joy invades your life as you realize that you are learning to abide in Christ.

Think About God's Word. Meditate on God's Word throughout the day. Focus your thoughts on the Bible. Think about who God is and what He has done. This takes time to learn, but Scripture offers a promise of God's prosperity in our lives when we meditate on His Word:

> His delight is in the law of the LORD,
>   and on his law he meditates day and night.
> He is like a tree planted by streams of water,
>   which yields its fruit in season
> and whose leaf does not wither.
>   Whatever he does prospers. (Psalm 1:2-3)

Rick Warren reminds us in *The Purpose-Driven Life,*

When you think about a problem over and over in your mind, that's called worry. When you think about God's Word over and over in your mind, that's meditation. If you know how to worry, you already know how to meditate! You just need to switch your attention from your problems to Bible verses.[2]

Do you want to move into a new place as a praying intercessor and practice God's presence even more than you ever did before? We are entering days when the Word of God in our hearts is going to be absolutely necessary. Don't worry—we can live above all that is happening here on earth if we keep in mind that everything we do can be spending time with God. We only need to be aware of His presence during the day, whatever we're doing. He wants to be invited into the center of our activities. As world conditions worsen, we will ride on high places above the storm. This is how we will defeat the Enemy. Practicing God's presence through short prayers and meditation will make all the difference. Together let's stay aware of His presence and step up higher, into a new realm of intimacy. Let's learn to rest in God's presence rather than worry.

Do not let this Book of the Law depart from your mouth; meditate on it day and night, so that you may be careful to do everything written in it. Then you will be prosperous and successful. Have I not commanded you? Be strong and courageous. Do not be terrified; do not be discouraged, for the Lord your God will be with you wherever you go.
— Joshua 1:8-9

A SUSTAINED PURSUIT AFTER GOD'S OWN HEART

The revelation David had about the emotions of God equipped his heart for a sustained, abandoned pursuit of God, through his many weaknesses and failures, as well as his stunning victories. David is the picture of the end time church, which will be a lovesick, worshipping warrior bride, and a people after God's own heart.
— Mike Bickle, "David's Paradigm of Enjoyable Prayer"

David was a man after God's own heart. He was moved by what moved the heart of God. He wanted to know how God felt about life. He wanted to be intimately acquainted with God's ways of doing things and why He did them. He wanted to be passionate toward God. David was after God's heartbeat for the world. God's desire is that we pursue Him with all of our hearts, just like David did, abandoning ourselves to His purposes and plans.

Are we eager as intercessors to study the heart of God? May God help us to know the secret of such a prayer life that is moved by a passionate, sustained pursuit of the heart, mind, and will of God.

When you and I know the emotions and feelings in God's heart, we can better obey Him. We can walk obediently in His Word and live radically for Him because His love sustains us. We are able to obey God in the long term when we are linked to His power rather than our own weakness. We can live joyfully because we are living in a whole new realm. Psalm 16:11 says, "You will fill me with joy in your presence."

I entered the mission field at a young age. Missionary life is filled with seasons of hardship and endurance. My first big lesson in this came when I lived on a missionary ship with people from all over the world. The name of the ship was *Doulos*, which means "servant" in Greek. Everyone was encouraged to be like Jesus, coming not to be served but to serve. My first job on the ship was to serve food to more than three hundred people from over forty different nations. That was not so difficult—until we set out to sea. Our first major voyage was sailing across the Atlantic Ocean, a two-week journey that I secretly anticipated with considerable fear and dread. After all, I was not a sailor. I couldn't even swim! How could I serve food during a rough voyage? And they predicted a rough voyage since it was hurricane season!

Sure enough, the trip got tempestuous. I remember one of my fellow dining room workers coming out of the kitchen holding a tray loaded with soft blocks of butter on little plates. Suddenly the ship lurched forward, and she completely lost her balance. Butter flew everywhere! It was on everything, including my coworker, the floor, and the tables. On another day, I was serving soup to all the tables in my row. I thought I was doing pretty well until I served a tall lanky guy, who then leaned over and emptied his stomach right in the middle of his bowl. I turned in the other direction and got out of there fast! Fortunately both incidents later turned into humorous stories, just a few of our many experiences at sea.

What sustained me in those early experiences of missionary life and all throughout my missionary career was seeing God's heartbeat for the world. It was a personal understanding of His heart and His love for me that got me through the day-in, day-out experiences of ship life. I was able to focus on God and His love during those times.

Without understanding the love of God, it is impossible to serve Him successfully for a long time overseas. Sooner or later the weaknesses in our lives and the heaviness of ministry demands catch up with us. When we pursue God's heart, everything becomes easier because we are walking with and focusing on God. We begin to comprehend His overwhelming love for us personally and the deep pleasure He has in our fellowship with Him. This motivates us to change. Our actions and lifestyles become more Christlike because we see ourselves the way God sees us, and this impacts everything we say and do. We see the beauty of God, and then we see ourselves through His eyes. This enables us to say no to sin and grow in holiness.

Eventually the truth about God and how He loves the entire world moves into our hearts. We then respond to God from our hearts. We experience the love of God in a deeper measure. But we must realize that Satan will always attack our relationship with Christ. He knows that this is the key to all fruitfulness and spiritual victory. When we know the love of God on a deep level, we can conquer any difficulty—even sea voyages. We can face any trial because we can trust our Father to know what is best for us. He will carry us through. He knows us intimately. We are His beloved children.

I believe strongly that one thing the devil seeks to do is to sneak in and subtly distract our attention from the purity and simplicity of loving God. He doesn't mind if we exalt revival, healing, or anything else, as long as we lose our focus on the simplicity of heart-level lavish devotion to the Son of God.
— Mike Bickle, "David's Paradigm of Enjoyable Prayer"

LONGINGS OF THE HEART

One of the most fundamental realities in the Spirit is that our Bridegroom King so desires, pursues and enjoys us as His Bride. When the human heart is assured through the revelation of the Spirit that we are deeply enjoyed, then something powerful is awakened within us. This is truly the beginning of our experience of the Divine romance.
— Mike Bickle, "The Bridal Paradigm"

We all have inner longings that can be met only in an intimate relationship with God. Men and women everywhere try to meet these longings in different ways but don't find fulfillment until they embrace the Lord and His salvation. We can never fully live for God, abandoned to His purposes, until we have the longings of our hearts met by His perfect love. When we have had a personal revelation of that love, knowing He deeply enjoys us and treasures our relationship with Him, we will be able to live and pray more effectively. The Holy Spirit will guide us in our praying and our "goings and doings." Our faith will deepen and prayer will grow from that fellowship with Him, becoming a greater joy and privilege.

We long for the assurance that God enjoys us. How few of us really know deep in our hearts that God enjoys us! How few of us know experientially that God feels our pain and knows our struggles.

He knows that we are sinners, and He has knowledge of our secrets.

He knows the dreams and intentions in our hearts.

He knows when we feel lonely and when no one understands us.

He alone understands the deep desires and longings in our hearts.

Despite our confusion and weaknesses, God loves us, enjoys us, and believes in us. He treats us with honor and walks through every day and hour with us. When we learn this truth, we are changed forever. Love begins to impact everything we do, including how we pray. We rise up with new confidence. Mike Bickle puts it this way in "The Bridal Paradigm":

> The absolute strongest emotion in our being is the craving to be assured that God enjoys us. The power of feeling enjoyed. We imagine God will enjoy us when we are

in heaven; we can even imagine God will enjoy us if we are spiritually mature on the earth. But the idea that He enjoys us while we are spiritually immature is unthinkable for many people.[3]

We long for the assurance that God enjoys us, and then we long to be captivated by God. We have a deep desire in our hearts to be excited and enthralled by the wonder and awe of who He is. We love beauty, and we long to be spiritually alive. We want to experience wonder. We are designed for it in the core of our being.

When I was in France, I saw a creative desire in the culture. You can see it in the architecture, fashions, beautiful gardens, and floral designs throughout the country. You can even see it in the way the French artistically plan and serve a meal. All of this points to a God-given craving deep inside the human heart that longs for beauty, something to treasure that is so precious a person would give everything to possess it. The apostle Paul was such a man. He was so captivated by God that he wrote in Philippians 3:8, "I consider everything a loss compared to the surpassing greatness of knowing Christ Jesus my Lord, for whose sake I have lost all things. I consider them rubbish, that I may gain Christ."

Because God designed us for fellowship with Him, we really do need to experience at the core of our being the awe and wonder of who He is. God wants to bring us to that place of wonder in His beauty and majesty. If we were to ask people about their relationship with the Lord, we would learn that the majority of Christians have not been fully captivated by Him. Many have simply gone through the motions of what it is to be a Christian.

This has to change.

We need supernatural strength in the inner person to be able to stand strong as the pressures increase on the earth. Those who have developed an intimate relationship with God will be able to stand strong and walk in His supernatural peace.

This is the time to practice His presence and develop friendship with our Bridegroom King.

This is the time to pursue His heart, becoming captivated by Him and His awesome majesty.

This is the time to grow in our faith.

The redeemed across the earth will one day see their Messiah as their heavenly Bridegroom. In the overflow of that revelation, we will redefine ourselves as the cherished Bride. This transforms our hearts and changes our lives. He will change the way that we view Him and therefore, the way we view ourselves. The deep spiritual void in our lives can be fulfilled in our heavenly Bridegroom.

— Mike Bickle, "The Bridal Paradigm"

PERSONAL APPLICATION

HOW TO GROW IN INTIMATELY KNOWING THE HEART OF GOD. As you seek to practice God's presence and pursue His heart, take several minutes each day this week to personally apply this truth to your own life. Read and meditate on Psalm 84; listen carefully, and let it speak to your heart. Pray this psalm back to God as a prayer. Try singing it to the Lord. You may want to pick different Scriptures each day, or you can concentrate on this psalm.

- Renew your mind in God's Word. We must know the Lord's Word because it will transform us and lead us into God's perfect will. "Do not conform any longer to the pattern of this world, but be transformed by the renewing of your mind. Then you will be able to test and approve what God's will is — his good, pleasing and perfect will" (Romans 12:2).
- Meditate on the Word. We must let God's Word permeate our hearts. We often move too quickly through life. We need to discipline ourselves to be still and know God. "I meditate on your precepts and consider your ways" (Psalm 119:15).
- Speak the Word back to the Lord in prayer. We need to learn to pray scriptural prayers back to God. Declaring scriptural promises establishes them in the spirit. "What

you decide on will be done, and light will shine on your ways" (Job 22:28).

- Sing the Word back to the Lord. Let God's Word move from head knowledge to heart knowledge. Making melody in your heart to God helps touch your feelings and brings satisfaction to your soul. "My soul will be satisfied as with the richest of foods; with singing lips my mouth will praise you" (Psalm 63:5).

HOW TO HELP OTHERS GROW IN INTIMACY WITH GOD. Get together with another person or group, and practice praying the Word back and forth together. Begin with the first verse of Psalm 84. You may want to first read the entire psalm together. Then begin to pray it verse by verse, letting God lead you as you pray. It will become more real as you speak it out in prayer to one another. As Paul reminded us, "Speak to one another with psalms, hymns and spiritual songs. Sing and make music in your heart to the Lord" (Ephesians 5:19).

MY PRAYER TO GOD

Lord, help me to practice Your presence and abide in Your love. "As the Father has loved me, so have I loved you. Now remain in my love" [John 15:9]. Teach me to meditate on Your Word throughout the day instead of my problems. Forgive me for when I worry instead of trust You. I want to be one who pursues Your heart as David did. Help me to pray Your Word and speak it to others. Awaken me, O God, to Your deep enjoyment of who I am. Give me revelation of Your beauty, give me joy in Your presence, and take me deeper in knowing You that I may be prepared for the coming days. Help me embrace You as my Bridegroom, King, and loving Father. Show me a greater dimension of Your love. Reveal to me Your transcendent beauty. Teach me to pray as one who abides in Your love always, deeply touched by Your deep longing for me. Like Paul, I want to know Your surpassing greatness [see Philippians 3:8]. In Jesus' name, amen.

CHAPTER TWO

THE INTERCESSOR AND FAITH

And without faith it is impossible to please God, because anyone who comes to him must believe that he exists and that he rewards those who earnestly seek him.
— Hebrews 11:6

OUR CAPTAIN'S LOUD, deep voice boomed over the public-address system: "Meet together in the main lounge immediately! We must pray and ask God to calm the seas!"

For several years, I lived aboard the *Doulos* as it sailed from country to country. On this occasion, we were sailing down the coast of South America and were about to enter the Strait of Magellan, a narrow passage just south of Chile. Our next port of ministry was the southernmost city of Punta Arenas at the tip of Chile. You could consider this area of the world literally the ends of the earth.

The straits are known for their treacherous seas. The pilot said we could not pass through unless the seas became calm. The weather was characteristically turbulent, which would make it difficult for our old ship to sail through safely. This ship, built in 1914, is in the *Guinness World Records* (as of 2007) as the oldest floating passenger ship in the world.

The entire staff and crew dropped whatever they were doing and quickly gathered in the main lounge. The captain urged us to pray that God would give us a safe passage through the Strait of Magellan so that we could arrive on time. Because of the seriousness of the situation, we needed prayers of faith for the impossible. We were absolutely dependent on God for our future on that vulnerable old ship. Only He could save our situation. We immediately gathered in small groups, praying fervently that God would calm the seas. Within minutes, God answered prayer: The seas became still, and the ship passed peacefully through the narrow passage.

I sat on deck at the bow of the ship with a young man, admiring the beauty of God's creation in this gorgeous part of the world. Actually, this was our first date—one we would always remember in the years after we married. During that passage through the Strait of Magellan, we saw many shipwrecks right in the midst of the natural beauty of massive rocks and clear blue seas. This was a vivid reminder of God's powerful answer to our desperate prayers. Are prayers of faith for the impossible effective? Yes! Our ship was able to reach its destination safely, and we were able to continue our conferences and evangelistic programs right on schedule. God used the situation to build our faith.

You may be asking, *How can I develop my faith in God? How can I pray for the impossible in my life circumstances? How do I tap into God's unlimited power when I feel so weak?* Let's discover how faith-filled prayers are developed through delay and how we can pray with faith for the impossible—even surrendering our weakness into God's strong supernatural power. Our dependence can actually open the way for God's unlimited opportunity to bless.

FAITH-FILLED PRAYERS DEVELOPED THROUGH DELAY

Faith does the impossible because it lets God undertake for us, and nothing is impossible for God. How great — without qualification or limitation — the power of faith is! If doubt can be banished from the heart and unbelief is made a stranger there, what we ask from God will surely come to pass. . . . Prayer throws faith on God and God on the world. Only God can move mountains, but faith and prayer move God.
— E. M. Bounds, *E. M. Bounds on Prayer*[1]

Are you trusting God for something bigger than yourself, for something that only God can do? Are you stepping out of your comfort zone, beyond what is normal in your sight, asking God for things that are God-sized and not man-sized? Are you filled with the plans and purposes of God, with an anticipation of what God will do if you believe and do not give up?

This is what God wants. We need to come to Him in faith with a great expectation of meeting with Him and seeing Him answer our prayers. Let us believe that God rewards faith and those who diligently seek Him (see Hebrews 11:6). Faith is the currency of heaven. The question we must ask is, "How can our faith be enlarged so that we have this currency of heaven?" One of the most significant ways is through delay.

Yet faith is often called upon to wait patiently before God and is prepared for God's seeming delays in answering prayer. Faith does not grow disheartened because prayer is not immediately honored. It takes God at His Word and lets Him take what time He chooses in fulfilling His purposes and in carrying on His work. There is bound to be delay and long days of waiting for true faith, but faith accepts the conditions.[2]

Jesus used delay in the interest of a greater good. Look at the story of the death of Lazarus (see John 11:1-44). The faith of Mary and Martha was tested. Jesus waited; Lazarus died. This was a seemingly impossible situation. What is more hopeless than death—not only physical death but death of all dreams, plans, and hopes? If God delays in answering your prayer, wait for Him. Waiting is not being lazy or going to sleep. It is not giving up. Rather, it is activity under command—being ready for when the command comes, and doing nothing until it comes. In His own good timing, God will give the command and break through all the obstacles. He will come and will not be late.

When starting the ministry of Intercessors Arise International, I ran into many difficulties. I knew what God wanted to do, but numerous obstacles came my way. Over and over again I ran into computer problems, and over and over again I had to lay them in God's hands and pray. The Enemy fought hard, and I finally made a decision to pray through all the obstacles and wait until God broke through. I knew in my heart that He wanted to raise up a vehicle to encourage intercession. It was a big test of my faith, a mountain that had to be conquered, and God broke through. It was an assignment in prayer that was too big for me but was conquerable for God. "'Have faith in God,' Jesus answered. . . . 'Therefore I tell you, whatever you ask for in prayer, believe that you have received it, and it will be yours'" (Mark 11:22,24).

God answered prayer, and now my faith has been enlarged to believe Him for much greater things regarding Intercessors Arise International. I believe that the test of faith was absolutely necessary for what God wanted to do. Whatever obstacle you are facing, whatever impossibility you are praying through, don't give up. God wants to enlarge your faith through the difficulty and the delay. Believe that one day He will break through in abundance. Thank Him now for what He will do even when you don't see it. Remember, faith is the assurance of things hoped for, the conviction of things not seen.

Delay is often the test and the strength of faith. How much patience is required when these times of testing come! Yet faith gathers strength by waiting and praying. Patience has its perfect work in the school of delay. In some instances, delay is of the very nature of the prayer. God has to do many things before He gives the final answer. There are things that are essential to the lasting good of the person who is requesting the favor from Him.

— E. M. Bounds, *E. M. Bounds on Prayer*[3]

PRAYERS OF FAITH FOR THE IMPOSSIBLE

A furious squall came up, and the waves broke over the boat, so that it was nearly swamped. Jesus was in the stern, sleeping on a cushion. The disciples woke him and said to him, "Teacher, don't you care if we drown?" He got up, rebuked the wind and said to the waves, "Quiet! Be still!" Then the wind died down and it was completely

calm. He said to his disciples, "Why are you so afraid? Do you still have no faith?" They were terrified and asked each other, "Who is this? Even the wind and the waves obey him!"
— Mark 4:37-41

Rarely are the waters in the North Sea calm. And there we were, off the coast of France passing right through the North Sea. The waters were stormy on the first day, and the high waves sent many of us to bed, seasick. When your cabin is bouncing to and fro and you feel as if you have the worst case of the flu, it is hard to imagine stillness, peace, and a sense of well-being. But we fervently prayed (just as we had in Chile), and God calmed the seas. It seemed impossible at the time, but to God all things are possible. God wants to answer prayers of faith for the impossible. Are we willing to step out into this dimension in our prayer lives?

What impossible assignments has God given you in prayer? Is it the salvation of a loved one, revival in your city or nation, healing from an illness? To you it may seem impossible (and the Devil would want you to believe that), but God loves to answer impossible prayers because He, the creator of all that is, lives in the realm of what seems impossible. He wants us to be obedient in prayer so that He can stretch our faith to the place where He dwells. In this place of faith-filled obedience, He makes the impossible possible, by His might and power alone. And He wraps His strength around our weakness, bringing our faith to a new level.

The first day at sea on this voyage was miserable for most of us, and we had three more days to endure. But God was at work realigning our lives with His, conquering in a small way the self-life so that His life could shine more brightly through, and strengthening us in faith by answering our prayers for calm seas. We all have a tendency to get discouraged at the enormity of the task before us, in the weariness of the battle when the storms of life seem overwhelming, and when we perceive our own inability to have strength or faith for what is ahead.

We must realize that we are not alone. God is powerful, and He is with us through every storm and danger in life. I once heard the story about a house that caught on fire one night and was being consumed with flames. A young boy was forced to climb out on the roof to escape. His father stood below with his arms outstretched, calling out loudly to his son, "Jump! I will catch you." The only way to save his life was to get the boy to jump. But he saw only the huge flames and black smoke and was terribly afraid. His father kept yelling frantically, "Jump! I will catch you." The boy fearfully protested, "Daddy, I can't see you. I can't see you," to which the father replied, "But I can see you, and that's all that matters."

God Desires Prayers of Faith. E. M. Bounds reminds us,

> Nothing can be clearer, or more distinct, more unlimited both in application and extent, than the plea and urgency of Christ, "Have faith in God" (Mark 11:22). Faith covers worldly as well as spiritual needs. Faith scatters excessive anxiety and needless care about what will be eaten, what will be drunk, what will be worn.[4]

God breaks through if we don't give up in prayer. Sometimes we feel the darkness of life just like that young boy on the roof. We can't see our way through a situation, but we pray fervently to God for the answer. We may say, "God, I can't feel Your presence. Are

You with me?" And He says to us, "I can see you, and that's all that matters. I will never leave you or forsake you. You can trust Me." We must realize that God is there and that He will catch us even though we can't see our way through. He will grant us victory step-by-step as we continue in prayer. Don't give up in prayer, because He will win the battle for you. Remember that His strength is made perfect in our weakness. Let us pray for one another that our faith may not fail. Faith honors God. He answers prayer according to our faith (see Matthew 9:29). We link our humanity to His omnipotence when we pray in faith.

I want to believe God for the supernatural in intercession, for the impossible to become possible, for His extraordinary hand of power in nations as well as in my life. I want to believe God for a mighty prayer movement that covers the earth. To do so, I need to be ready to take action according to God's direction.

Last year God opened the door to start a one-month 24/7 House of Prayer in southern Spain. It was a step of faith. We invited intercessors from several nations to join us. We invited the churches of southern Spain to join us. God provided a hotel for this month of day-and-night prayer. He blessed us in a marvelous way. Everyone grew in his or her prayer life, and we were able to keep the prayer room going day and night. This vision expanded to pray not only for Spain but for North Africa as well. This led to another one-month 24/7 House of Prayer on the east coast of the United States. We now have invitations to do this in France, Austria, and other nations. It all began with prayers of faith and an obedient step of faith in Spain.

Nothing Is Impossible for God. Elijah, prophet of God, stood before King Ahab and announced that there would be no rain unless he said so. And a drought set in (see 1 Kings 17). For three years, crops withered in the fields, and livestock died of thirst. And when it was time, God sent word through Elijah that it would rain once again.

Leonard Ravenhill, a prominent British evangelist, wrote,

Such praying men are always our national benefactors. Elijah was such. He had heard a voice, seen a vision, tasted a power, measured an enemy, and with God as partner, wrought a victory. He knew the mind of God. Therefore he, one man, strangled a nation and altered the course of nature. By the key of faith, which fits every lock, Elijah locked heaven, pocketed the key, and made Ahab tremble. Though it is wonderful indeed when God lays hold of a man, earth can know one greater wonder—when a man lays hold of God.[5]

May we be men and women of faith who lay hold of God in prayer as Elijah did. It will take fervent prayers of faith for the seemingly impossible task ahead. Prayers are needed to turn nations toward God, to penetrate countries and people groups with the gospel, and to see strongholds in our cities pulled down by the power of the name of Jesus, thereby opening doors to bring in the lost. God majors on performing what men often see as the impossible. He loves to break through when all hope seems dim.

God can calm the stormy seas in your personal life, family, city, and nation. He longs to do the impossible in answering the cries of intercession. Prayer is the avenue to see all needs met. Prayer and faith go together. Ask God for increased faith in prayer for all believers. We see in Luke 17:5 that the disciples wanted more faith and prayed, "Increase our faith!" We need great faith and aggressive prayer for all the nations of the world. First Corinthians 16:13 says, "Stand firm in the faith." May we look back on these days and say as Paul did in 2 Thessalonians 1:3, "Your faith is growing more and more."

Don't discount what is possible with God (Philippians 4:13). When God gives an assignment, it is no longer an impossibility, but rather it is an absolute certainty. When God gives you a seemingly impossible task, the only thing preventing it from coming to pass is your disobedience. . . . How do you respond to assignments that seem impossible? Do you write them off as unattainable? Or do you immediately adjust your life to God's revelation, watching with anticipation to see how He will accomplish His purposes through your obedience. God wants to do the impossible through your life.
— Henry and Richard Blackaby, *Experiencing God, Day-by-Day*

DEPENDENCE — GOD'S UNLIMITED OPPORTUNITY TO BLESS

As a child of God, you ought to expect God to answer your prayers. Do you ask God to do something without adjusting your life to what you are praying? If you are praying for revival, how are you preparing for its coming? If you are praying for forgiveness, are you still living with guilt? If you have asked God to provide for your needs, do you remain worried and anxious? Ask God to increase your faith, and then begin living a life that reflects absolute trust in Him.
— Henry and Richard Blackaby, *Experiencing God, Day-by-Day*

We all want God to answer our prayers; we believe in the power of prayer. But when it comes down to our own individual lives and problems, we often don't have the faith to believe that God will answer. Unbelief and independence trap us. But God wants to enlarge our territory. He wants to bless us with increase, because His nature is to bless. Our lack of faith and our fear of stepping out in dependence on God are what get in the way. The truth is, the things we do for God should be outside of our own abilities; they should be evidence we are trusting in His supernatural ability. When we back away from dependence, we are not living by faith. We need to be willing to attempt things big enough that unless God steps in, we are sure to fail. Faith is like jumping out of an airplane at fifteen thousand feet or sailing across an ocean in the oldest floating passenger ship in the world. If God doesn't catch you, you will fall or drown. But how do you know unless you jump? This is the kind of faith and dependence He is looking for in our lives.

Remember the prayer of Jabez in 1 Chronicles 4:10: "Jabez cried out to the God of Israel, 'Oh, that you would bless me and enlarge my territory! Let your hand be with me, and keep me from harm so that I will be free from pain.' And God granted his request." Jabez cried out to God to enlarge his territory and bless him. He cried out for God's hand to be with him. Jabez was greatly blessed by God because he didn't let obstacles become larger than his faith. He knew the character of God and knew that God loved to bless. We, too, are made for destiny. We have a God-inspired desire to impact our world. Created for something bigger than ourselves, we are designed to touch a lost world. We long to make an impact on our land for eternity, whether it is where we work, live, or minister.

But in reality, most of us are afraid to step out by faith.

An African antelope called the impala can jump to over ten feet high and over a distance of thirty feet! But you can keep impalas from escaping with only a three-foot-high stone wall. They can't see where they will land on the other side of the wall, so they won't even try to jump it. In the same way, we often won't try anything we can't see because we are locked in by our fears. Faith is the ability to trust God even when we cannot see. Faith frees us to trust God who has all the resources of heaven. Why are we afraid to become dependent on a God who has unlimited resources? God has all the resources in the world. His power is limitless. He wants to bless us, but we must have faith. If we pray for God to enlarge our borders, we must depend on Him and prepare to believe for miracles that only God can bring about.

God gives us the desires of our hearts, and He wants to answer extraordinary prayers combined with extraordinary faith. He wants us to live beyond our self-imposed limits. He wants to give us favor, but many of us don't believe it. I encourage you to begin to pray big prayers, because God is able to bless.

I realize that I must demonstrate my dependence on God continually by stepping out by faith in whatever way He leads. And then I watch Him perform the miracle. Bruce Wilkinson says the following:

> The most exhilarating miracles in my life have always started with a bold request to expand God's kingdom a lot. When you take little steps, you don't need God. It's when you thrust yourself in the mainstream of God's plan for this world—which are beyond our ability to

accomplish — and plead with Him, Lord, use me — give me more ministry for You — that you release miracles.[6]

My willingness and weakness offered to God's will and supernatural power result in God's unlimited opportunity to bless. God is trying to teach each one of us dependence on His strong hand and supernatural power.

A small group of scientists were searching for an extremely rare flower in the Himalayan Mountains. After a long search, they found it, but it was growing on the side of a very steep cliff and they had no way to get it. They finally had an idea and asked a young boy if they could lower him over the cliff on a rope to get it. They offered him a bribe that was quite big in the eyes of that small boy. But the cliff was scary and extremely dangerous. The boy thought for a minute and suddenly told the scientists to wait a minute, and he ran home. Finally he returned again with an older man. He told them that if they let his father hold on to the rope, he would allow them to lower him over the side of the cliff. He knew that his father would protect him.

This example is similar to our relationship with God, our heavenly Father. If God is holding the rope, we can trust Him completely with our lives. We know He will not let go.

When we surrender our weakness into the mighty hand of God, our needs and problems turn into His unlimited opportunity. Then God becomes great through us. Then He can entrust us with an enlarged territory and the fulfillment of His plan for us. But we have to take steps of faith, even if they are small. God honors these steps and turns them into His unlimited opportunity because at that very point, we become dependent on Him. This is

His plan for our lives. If we are willing to give God our weakness and obey His Word by faith, then it opens the door for supernatural power and God's opportunity to bless.

What step of faith is God asking you to take today? Will you put everything into His almighty hands, adjust your life to what you are praying for, and step out by faith in whatever way He leads? When you do this, you become dependent in His dependable hands. He is waiting for your invitation to enlarge your faith.

If seeking God's blessing is our ultimate act of worship, and asking to do more for Him is our utmost ambition, then asking for God's hand upon us is our strategic choice to sustain and continue the great things that God has begun in our lives. That's why you could call God's hand on you "the touch of greatness." You do not become great; you become dependent on the strong hand of God. Your surrendered need turns into His unlimited opportunity. And He becomes great through you.

— Bruce Wilkinson, *The Prayer of Jabez*

PERSONAL APPLICATION

HOW TO GROW IN A LIFE OF FAITH. It is time to evaluate your personal faith life. Answer the following questions carefully and prayerfully.

- How is God presently testing my faith?
- In what way does God want to enlarge my territory?
- What impossible assignment has God given me in prayer?
- In what way am I trusting God for something bigger than myself? How am I stepping out of my comfort zone?
- In what way am I waiting in faith for God to do something? Am I patiently waiting during the delay?
- How am I surrendering my weakness — needs and problems — into His mighty hand?
- In what way is God teaching me to depend on His strength and supernatural power?

Write a prayer to God bringing your test of faith (impossible assignment, personal weaknesses, desires, or dreams) before Him and laying them in His mighty hands. In your prayer, include your answers to the questions in the preceding list.

HOW TO HELP OTHERS GROW IN FAITH. Get together with another person or group and ask God to lead you. Then together answer the questions from "How to Grow in a Life of Faith" one by one. This could take more than one meeting time, so consider answering only two or three of the questions per week and bring in Bible verses to study relating to the questions. At the end of each session, pray together and ask God to build your faith and help you to patiently wait, step out of your comfort zone, enlarge your territory, depend on Him, and so on. These questions can lead you into a deep discussion with truthful sharing that can be life-transforming.

MY PRAYER TO GOD

Lord, I ask You to enlarge my faith [see 2 Thessalonians 1:3, NASB]. In difficult circumstances in my life, please remove doubt and help me to stand firm in my faith [see 1 Corinthians 16:13] and faithfully pray through [name impossible prayer assignments]. Give me a supernatural faith to believe You and to fix my eyes upon You instead of the storms around me. I want to believe You for marvelous breakthroughs in [name your situation] for Your honor and glory. I ask to be a person who has faith in the impossible. I ask You to give me faith-filled prayers. I pray that You would bless me and enlarge my territory. Let Your hand be with me and keep me from harm [see 1 Chronicles 4:10]. Break every area of unbelief in my life. Increase my faith to believe that You will answer my prayers [see Mark 11:24]. Help me to spread faith everywhere I go. Thank You that even the wind and the waves obey You. In Jesus' name, amen.

CHAPTER THREE

THE INTERCESSOR AND CHARACTER

The prayer of a righteous man is powerful and effective.

— James 5:16

I LEFT MY country with fear and anxiety as I stepped into the airplane. My husband and I were going to India, and I knew in my heart that it would not be an easy trip. I had traveled to more than sixty countries and had lived overseas as a missionary for many years—why was I so concerned about *this* time?

The Lord had impressed on me that this trip would include brokenness and suffering. I had wanted to go to the poorest place on earth and feel what they felt. I knew God wanted to do something supernatural in me. It was time for something deeper to happen.

After a three-day delay in Amsterdam, we finally arrived in New Delhi. Reaching our ministry destinations inevitably meant hours of traveling over bumpy roads. Sometimes we were able to go only fifteen miles per hour because of huge potholes. Once we took a wrong turn that added four more hours to our trip! Each day I thanked God when we reached our destination in one piece and were able to minister to the church in that town or village.

After long hours of travel and delays, we arrived at a village where a group of women eagerly waited to hear me speak. I stood up in the church building and looked across the sea of faces. The women sat cross-legged on the floor, dressed in colorful saris absolutely beautiful against their darker skin. Suddenly I felt such a sense of holiness in that room. These women were the poorest of the poor, owning absolutely nothing. There I was, from one of the richest countries, having everything anyone could ever want. Yet as I looked at the faces of these women, I was touched deeply by their simplicity and brokenness, by their Christlike love and joy, by their gentle hearts and holy character.

I began to tell them how God was going to use them in revival in India. I began to share how they had so much to teach me, a woman from the West. And then I began to weep, which I don't do often, so I knew that God was doing something special in me. I wept because they who understood brokenness and suffering had so much to teach me. I was privileged to be in their presence.

Suddenly the women began to cry. My brokenness touched them profoundly, and they responded. Every barrier between the rich and the poor, between those who have and those who have not, was shattered in an instant, and we were all one in Jesus. My translator excitedly said to me, "Something is happening. Indians don't usually hug, but these women want to hug you." So one by one I hugged each lady. As we embraced, they cried loudly and I sensed a deep love between us that will last through all eternity.

My life changed that day.

I saw true character demonstrated in humility, pure and simple.

I now see the poor as ones God is going to greatly use because they are rich in faith and character. And I was motivated in a new way to seek godly character because this is what God desires in our lives.

How can we grow in godly character? How can the words we say and the way we live demonstrate holiness and humility? How does our character affect the way we pray? When we discover the beauty of humility and brokenness and learn how our tongue can bring grace into the lives of others, we also discover joy in the secret place that breaks through into fruitful and effective prayer.

A HUMBLE HEART

God puts a great price on humility of heart. It is good to be clothed with humility as with a garment. It is written, "God resists the proud, but gives grace to the humble" (James 4:6). That which brings the praying soul near to God is humility of heart. That which gives wings to prayer is lowliness of mind. . . . Pride, self-esteem, and self-praise effectually shut the door of prayer. He who would come to God must approach the Lord with self hidden from his eyes.

— E. M. Bounds, *E. M. Bounds on Prayer*[1]

Walking in humility is essential for those who want to touch the world through prayer. I was touched deeply by the humility I saw in the Christians in India. Now God reminds me over and over again to pray, "Lord, give me a humble heart." None of us can change the world unless we have a humble heart and walk in the very humility in which Jesus walked. He became nothing. We don't really understand the depths of humility that He walked in while here on earth. He died an agonizing, undeserved death for our salvation. We are so filled with pride, but Jesus emptied Himself.

A young seminary student was excited about preaching his first sermon in his home church. He felt very prepared after three years in seminary, and when he got up to preach, he walked boldly and confidently to the pulpit with his head held high. As he read the Scriptures, he began to lose his concentration and panicked. He forgot his sermon and quickly ended his message, prayed, and sat down with his head bent over. Later one of the godly men in his church whispered to him, "If you had gone up to the pulpit the way you came down, you would have come down the way you went up."

This is so true for all of us. If we walk in humility instead of pride, then God will raise us up and use us for His glory. He resists the proud but gives grace to the humble (see James 4:6), "for everyone who exalts himself will be humbled, and he who humbles himself will be exalted" (Luke 18:14).

Am I willing to go through pain, misunderstanding, and brokenness for Him as He did for us? I was so challenged by the poor in spirit that my outlook on life has been radically affected. I want that spirit of humility I saw in those Indian Christians. May God give us a revelation of how essential humility is for effective prayer and intercession. Isaiah 57:15 says,

> *For this is what the high and lofty One says—*
> *he who lives forever, whose name is holy:*
> *"I live in a high and holy place,*
> *but also with him who is contrite and lowly in spirit,*

to revive the spirit of the lowly
and to revive the heart of the contrite."

Pride is the big "I" of self. What is brokenness and humility? It is the painful, humiliating "Not I, but Christ" and "Not my will, but Yours be done." There is no self-exaltation in humility. It is lowly in heart and poor in spirit. You and I can choose to walk in this spirit. We only have to pray, "Lord, give me a humble heart that I might fear Your name. Clothe me in Your robe of humility, and take away all that does not please You." Let God touch your heart deeply as you grow in intercession. Let Jesus clothe you with this beautiful gift of humility so that He may release powerful prayers through you for all the downcast, poor, and brokenhearted around the world.

The Path to Brokenness. What are the ways God brings brokenness into our lives? Jesus is our example, having the attitude of a servant and humbling Himself on a cross.

Do nothing out of selfish ambition or vain conceit, but in humility consider others better than yourselves. Each of you should look not only to your own interests, but also to the interests of others.

Your attitude should be the same as that of Christ Jesus:

Who, being in very nature God,
did not consider equality with God something to be grasped,
but made himself nothing,
taking the very nature of a servant,

being made in human likeness.
And being found in appearance as a man,
he humbled himself
and became obedient to death—even death on a
cross! (Philippians 2:3-8)

God often uses His Word to break us. When we are confronted with His living Word, we see our own failures in light of His purity, and we are humbled. Jesus is a stone to make men stumble. "He who falls on this stone will be broken" (Matthew 21:44).

Brokenness also comes through pain and suffering. Paul's thorn in the flesh is a good example of this. Suffering brings forth godly character if we handle it correctly. Romans 5:3-4 says, "We . . . rejoice in our sufferings, because we know that suffering produces perseverance; perseverance, character; and character, hope."

Brokenness and humility come when we see where our own way has taken us. Sin shows us where we have fallen short of God's best:

I know my transgressions,
and my sin is always before me. (Psalm 51:3)

The Word of God, suffering, and seeing our own sin are ways God will lead us through the path to brokenness. Think about how He may be teaching you brokenness and humility.

The Character Traits of Brokenness. What do broken people look like? The following are some character traits of those who are broken. Use this list to carefully evaluate your own life.

- They don't defend themselves. They trust God to defend. "Do not take revenge, my friends, but leave room for God's wrath, for it is written: 'It is mine to avenge; I will repay,' says the Lord" (Romans 12:19).
- They are ready to be honest about themselves. "If we claim to be without sin, we deceive ourselves and the truth is not in us. If we confess our sins, he is faithful and just and will forgive us our sins and purify us from all unrighteousness" (1 John 1:8-9).
- They quickly admit they have sinned. Pride will deny that there is the possibility to sin. "Against you, you only, have I sinned and done what is evil in your sight" (Psalm 51:4).
- They are ready to make restitution. "If you are offering your gift at the altar and there remember that your brother has something against you, leave your gift there in front of the altar. First go and be reconciled to your brother; then come and offer your gift" (Matthew 5:23-24).
- They are convinced of their inability to serve God on their own. They realize their dependence on prayer because they know they can do nothing without God. "Create in me a pure heart, O God, and renew a steadfast spirit within me" (Psalm 51:10).
- They are able to rejoice and weep with others. They have compassion on the broken in the world and are able to enter into their pain. "Rejoice with those who rejoice; mourn with those who mourn" (Romans 12:15).

If you want to know what a person is really like, find out what makes him or her laugh and weep. A person who knows true brokenness knows how to do both. A comedian was entertaining at a hospital that specialized in rehabilitating polio victims and people with other extreme handicaps. This man was there to make the patients laugh regardless of their illness. He was able to do this with great success, but suddenly he left the platform and went to the restroom. Another man quickly followed to see if he was okay. He found him leaning against the wall sobbing like a child. But in a few minutes, the comedian regained his composure and appeared back on the platform to make the patients laugh again.

This man had godly character. He was broken over the suffering of those patients, but he also understood how to minister to them. We also need to have a broken heart and realize when to laugh and when to cry with those around us.

The Blessings of Brokenness. What does brokenness produce in us?

- **True humility.** "The sacrifices of God are a broken spirit; a broken and contrite heart, O God, you will not despise" (Psalm 51:17).
- **Spiritual fruit.** "I tell you the truth, unless a kernel of wheat falls to the ground and dies, it remains only a single seed. But if it dies, it produces many seeds" (John 12:24).
- **Healing.** "He heals the brokenhearted and binds up their wounds" (Psalm 147:3).
- **Closeness to God.** "The LORD is close to the brokenhearted and saves those who are crushed in spirit" (Psalm 34:18).

Humility is a rare Christian grace of great price in the courts of heaven, entering into and being an inseparable condition of effectual praying. It gives access to God when other qualities fail. . . . Its full portrait is found only in the Lord Jesus. Our prayers must be set low before they can ever rise high.
— E. M. Bounds, *E. M. Bounds on Prayer*[2]

WORDS THAT UPLIFT AND BRING GRACE

The Bible stresses that what you say is an accurate indication of what is in your heart. If your words bless and encourage others, they give evidence of a compassionate heart. If you often share the good news about Christ, you demonstrate a heart that is grateful for your own salvation. When others are in a crisis, do they know they will find peace and comfort in your words? Do you frequently and spontaneously offer prayers for others? Do your words and the manner in which you say them reveal a patient heart? All of these behaviors indicate a heart that is like the heart of the Father.
— Henry and Richard Blackaby, *Experiencing God, Day-by-Day*

The words we use have tremendous power. The Bible says that life and death are in the power of the tongue (see Proverbs 18:21). I believe that our prayers will have more power and a greater anointing when our everyday life is filled with words that uplift and bring grace to others (see Ephesians 4:29). There is no question that a holy life is a powerful life when it comes to seeing answers to prayer. Jesus' prayers were heard because of His reverent submission (see Hebrews 5:7). Righteous living and right speech come from a right heart before God. It is important for all of us who want to have an effective prayer life to carefully watch our speech.

The Power of the Tongue. A person can speak many words a minute and several thousand in an hour. You can imagine how many words an average person speaks in a day! And some estimates are that women speak twice as many words a day as men! We could fill a library in a lifetime! If we did, what would the titles of those books be? The tongue has a powerful influence on others. God is looking for a holy life, and one of the key areas that we must guard with all diligence is our tongue.

The truth is, we all have problems with what we say. That's probably why the Bible says so much about the tongue. Proverbs is filled with verses about both the positive and negative aspects of the tongue. I counted the terms *tongue*, *lips*, *mouth*, and *words*, and they appear over 170 times in the Bible. James 3:4-5 says, "Take ships as an example. Although they are so large and are driven by strong winds, they are steered by a very small rudder wherever the pilot wants to go. Likewise the tongue is a small part of the body, but it makes great boasts. Consider what a great forest is set on fire by a small spark."

Speaking negatively is costly in the spiritual realm, while watching what we say can bring spiritual reward. In Jericho, God's people marched around the city in silence for six days. When they finally shouted on the seventh day, the walls came down immediately. Their silence and then shouting at the right time won them the victory. This is true of us individually as well. If we guard our speech, we can win a great victory.

When we walk in the power of the Holy Spirit, we defeat the Enemy.

When we abide in Christ, His Spirit can flow from our lives in word and deed everywhere we go.

When we enter a place where fear is evident, we can come in the spirit of peace. We can speak words of peace.

Where there is hate, we can come in the spirit of love and kindness.

Our words can be kind and full of love. Our actions demonstrate love even in the midst of our enemies. We read in Galatians 5:22-23, "The fruit of the Spirit is love, joy, peace, patience, kindness, goodness, faithfulness, gentleness and self-control."

The Lips of the Righteous. In Proverbs 10, we find seven characteristics of the lips of the righteous. When we refrain from critical and negative speech, we must replace it with uplifting, positive, and grace-filled words. Think about the words you speak. Are they uplifting and do they bring life to others? Ask God to help you evaluate your speech as you read these verses:

- **A fountain of life.** "The mouth of the righteous is a fountain of life, but violence overwhelms the mouth of the wicked" (verse 11).
- **Discerning lips.** "Wisdom is found on the lips of the discerning, but a rod is for the back of him who lacks judgment" (verse 13).
- **Holds his tongue.** "When words are many, sin is not absent, but he who holds his tongue is wise" (verse 19).
- **Choice silver.** "The tongue of the righteous is choice silver, but the heart of the wicked is of little value" (verse 20).
- **Nourishes many.** "The lips of the righteous nourish many, but fools die for lack of judgment" (verse 21).
- **Brings forth wisdom.** "The mouth of the righteous brings forth wisdom, but a perverse tongue will be cut out" (verse 31).

- **Knows what is fitting.** "The lips of the righteous know what is fitting, but the mouth of the wicked only what is perverse" (verse 32).

On my trip to India, I took with me a book to read called *A Chance to Die*, by Elisabeth Elliot about Amy Carmichael. She was a successful missionary in India who saved children out of child prostitution, a shining example of one who had learned to give up her own life and live for God alone. Amy had godly character. Every time I rode on those bumpy roads or had to go through hardship, I said to myself, *This is a chance to die to myself.* I had many opportunities on that trip to remind myself again what God was doing inside me. He was teaching me humility and brokenness and developing my character. I was reminded in those moments to watch my tongue and speak words that would bless and uplift others. And when I did speak positively, God blessed even in the midst of hardship. When you're going through adversity, tell yourself, *I will watch the words that come out of my mouth. This is a chance to die to myself and live for Jesus.*

Jesus spoke plainly about our idle words, yet His warning often goes unheeded. Jesus said that for every idle word there will be a time of accounting in the day of judgment. We would expect Jesus to condemn profane and vile uses of the tongue, but idle words? Idle words are things we say carelessly, without concern for their impact on others. We too quickly assume that the sins of our tongue are minor sins, sins that God will overlook. Yet Jesus was fully aware of the devastating nature of our words.
— Henry and Richard Blackaby, *Experiencing God, Day-by-Day*

JOYFUL IN PRAYER

Rejoice in the Lord always. I will say it again: Rejoice! Let your gentleness be evident to all. The Lord is near. Do not be anxious about anything, but in everything, by prayer and petition, with thanksgiving, present your requests to God.
— Philippians 4:4-6

Is it truly possible to rejoice in the Lord always?

Paul says twice in Philippians 4:4 that we should do this. He knows that it's something we have to command and encourage ourselves to practice. We all struggle, and it's not fun. But Paul sets the bar high: While in prison, he rejoiced! And then he tells us to pray about everything with thanksgiving as we present our requests to God. Perhaps prayer is a key to the ability to rejoice always. It certainly is not easy to rejoice in certain circumstances of life, but we have a choice of how we will view those circumstances. God has an answer for everything, even when we don't see it through our human eyes. He knows the beginning from the end, and it's our choice if we want to link with Him or not. The world is negative and tries to squeeze us into its mold, but God has a way that we can walk through our circumstances victoriously.

Joy is a fruit of the Spirit. It is not something we can create ourselves — it comes from God. It's supernatural and persists in a deep, abiding way, even when we are in the midst of hardship. Joy is not the absence of pain or difficult circumstances. What could be harder than a Roman prison? But rejoicing always is learning to let God's Spirit fill you with His unquenchable joy, regardless of your circumstances. If you're joyful, your life becomes a testimony of Christ's light for a world looking desperately for hope.

Joy in the Secret Place of Prayer. I cannot tell you the number of times I have walked into a prayer meeting burdened with the cares of everyday life only to discover an unquenchable joy in God's presence. Often as I pray with others or silently wait upon God, I experience a joy that no circumstances can destroy. In 2005, I was diagnosed with breast cancer. This totally unexpected diagnosis initially threw me into deep darkness and discouragement. My entire future was threatened. But in the place of prayer in God's presence, I found hope even while going through cancer. I cannot begin to describe God's sustaining power and joy in the midst of a life-threatening illness. His joy is real and far deeper than any earthshaking life experience. I thank God for my experience with cancer, because through it God was able to develop a more Christlike character in my life. Now I am cancer-free, and I have a new appreciation for life.

Choosing to pray is not always easy, but it is the true path of life. Psalm 16:11 says,

> *You have made known to me the path of life;*
> *you will fill me with joy in your presence,*
> *with eternal pleasures at your right hand.*

There is joy in the secret place of prayer. There is joy as we choose to center our life in God and knowing Him. There is joy and breakthrough even in the darkest of circumstances when we choose to make Jesus our highest ambition, our deepest desire, and our greatest goal. Then He breaks through for us with transcending peace and supernatural understanding. Henry and Richard Blackaby remind us,

Jesus did not pray that you would be merely happy or even that you would escape grief. He prayed that you would have the same joy that the Father had given Him: a divine joy, a joy that comes from a deep and unwavering relationship with the Father. It is a joy that is grounded so firmly in a relationship with God that no change in circumstances could ever shake it. This is the kind of joy that Christ is praying will be in you.[3]

Destroyers of Joyful and Effective Prayer. The Enemy uses destroyers of effective prayer to try to diminish our power in intercession. He hates the secret place of prayer. In the book of Philippians, Paul recognizes these strategies of the Enemy and gives practical advice for how we might respond to them. It would be good for us to evaluate ourselves so that we may guard diligently against these thieves of our prayers. Here's what Paul has to say about some of the ways the Enemy uses to steal our joy and diminish our effectiveness in prayer:

- **Anxiety.** "Do not be anxious about anything, but in everything, by prayer and petition, with thanksgiving, present your requests to God. And the peace of God, which transcends all understanding, will guard your hearts and your minds in Christ Jesus" (4:6-7).
- **Self-righteousness.** "Be found in him, not having a righteousness of my own that comes from the law, but that which is through faith in Christ — the righteousness that comes from God and is by faith" (3:9).

- **Disagreements and poor relationships.** "I plead with Euodia and I plead with Syntyche to agree with each other in the Lord" (4:2).
- **Difficult circumstances.** "I am not saying this because I am in need, for I have learned to be content whatever the circumstances" (4:11).
- **Wrong thinking.** "Whatever is true, whatever is noble, whatever is right, whatever is pure, whatever is lovely, whatever is admirable — if anything is excellent or praiseworthy — think about such things" (4:8).
- **Lack of confidence.** "I can do everything through him who gives me strength" (4:13).
- **Complaining.** "Do everything without complaining or arguing, so that you may become blameless and pure, children of God without fault in a crooked and depraved generation, in which you shine like stars in the universe" (2:14-15).
- **Selfish ambition.** "Do nothing out of selfish ambition or vain conceit, but in humility consider others better than yourselves" (2:3).
- **Bad attitudes.** "Your attitude should be the same as that of Christ Jesus: Who, being in very nature God, did not consider equality with God something to be grasped, but made himself nothing, taking the very nature of a servant, being made in human likeness" (2:5-7).
- **Pride.** "Being found in appearance as a man, he humbled himself and became obedient to death — even death on a cross!" (2:8).

Don't be satisfied with a joyless life. There ought to be in every Christian a deep, settled fullness of the joy of Christ that no circumstance of life can dispel. This comes as you allow the Holy Spirit to express Himself in your life. One of the fruits of the Spirit is joy (Galatians 5:22). This joy is unlike any happiness that is produced by the world. It fills you and permeates everything you do.

— Henry and Richard Blackaby, *Experiencing God, Day-by-Day*

PERSONAL APPLICATION

HOW TO DEVELOP CHRISTLIKE CHARACTER. As you begin this exercise, sit quietly before the Lord for five minutes and ask Him to speak to you. Read the book of Philippians, and then do the following:

- Read carefully the destroyers of joyful and effective prayer. Let the Holy Spirit convict you of any sin.
- Be real, and refuse to hide from conviction of sin. Don't hide from ways you have personally diminished true effectiveness in prayer in your own life. Write down any ways you have lost joy in prayer using the list of destroyers of joyful and effective prayer. Be specific.
- Confess these sins before the Lord. Ask Him to remind you quickly whenever you fall into any of these sinful patterns. Receive His forgiveness (see 1 John 1:9).
- Ask God to make you joyful, effective, and fruitful in the secret place of prayer! Read "My Prayer to God" (at the end of the application).

HOW TO HELP OTHERS DEVELOP CHRISTLIKE CHARACTER. Meet with another individual or a small group and review this chapter together. Pray for God to speak to you as a group. Read the book of Philippians together. Read through the list of destroyers of joyful and effective prayer. Pray as a group, repenting of ways you have destroyed joy and effectiveness in your prayers. For instance, say,

"Lord, please forgive me for being anxious and worrying about [name the sin]. Help me to trust in You." When you feel that you are finished, begin a time of prayer asking God to make you joyful, effective, and fruitful in prayer. You may want to end with a time of worship and read the following prayer using "we" and "us" instead of "I" and "me."

MY PRAYER TO GOD

Lord, I pray that I would walk in Your righteousness and that my mouth would be a fountain of life to those in need [see Proverbs 10:11]. I pray for discerning lips and that You would give me the ability to hold my tongue [see Proverbs 10:19]. I ask that my prayers and words would be as choice silver. Give me the perfect words for a given situation. Let my words nourish many and bring forth Your wisdom. Help me speak what is fitting for every moment. I choose to guard my tongue. I choose to lift others up with my words. I choose words of life rather than death. Enable me to live a godly life.

Free me, Lord, from all of those things that steal my joy and from an ineffective prayer life. Give me joy in the secret place. Give me new insight, confidence, and faith in my prayers. Help me to walk in purity and humility. You are my righteousness and peace. Teach me contentment in the difficult circumstances that I face. I long for Your attitude of selfless giving and choose not to complain about anything. Help me to think only on that which is true, noble, right, pure, lovely, admirable, excellent, and praiseworthy. I desire to walk in Your joy and to rejoice in

You always in both good and difficult times. Help me to abide in the secret place with You. In Jesus' name, amen.

CHAPTER FOUR

THE INTERCESSOR AND STILLNESS

Be still, and know that I am God; I will be exalted among the nations, I will be exalted in the earth.

— Psalm 46:10

ABSOLUTELY BREATHTAKING.

Waking up early in the morning, going out on deck, having the wind blowing in your face, and smelling the fresh sea is an exhilarating experience. Watching the sunrise in all its brilliance, the beautiful colors shining against the luscious blue-green ocean — it's beyond description. When I joined the largest floating bookstore in the world that sailed from nation to nation, I hadn't quite anticipated the learning experience of a home at sea. But I gained some of my most important lessons in prayer during those voyages as I waited upon God.

During those days at sea, I began to learn the secret of silence and listening to God's still, small voice. What I first thought was a great loss of time turned into one of the greatest gains in my life. God began to show me the beauty of stillness and that everything in life depends on the cultivation of that one central place where we develop our relationship with Him. And I learned that my maximum effectiveness in prayer would come through those times of waiting.

During my first two-week sea voyage, I wrote this in my journal:

> There is great power in stillness. "In quietness and confidence shall be your strength." To receive great blessing from the Holy Spirit, there must be great preparation. For me the Atlantic voyage was a time of sleep and seasickness and seeing God in a brand-new way. It was a quiet time—a time of prayer and Bible memorization, a time of dependence, a time of adventure, a time of togetherness, a time of waiting, a time of endurance, and a time of stepping into the unknown. The ocean is truly a beautiful place, and God speaks in a special way out at sea when all other thoughts are lost in His majesty and might. "The earth is the LORD's, and everything in it, the world, and all who live in it; for he founded it upon the seas and established it upon the waters" (Psalm 24:1-2).

You don't have to live on a ship to learn the lessons of stillness. It's important for all of us to ask, *How can I learn to wait on God and hear His voice? How do I learn to be still and quiet even though my world is so busy?* Let's explore how to wait upon God, soak in His presence, and find ways to cultivate a listening ear to hear God's voice.

MAXIMUM EFFECTIVENESS THROUGH WAITING ON GOD

We experience the adventure of intercession to the degree we have learned to wait on God. Everything about our human nature rebels against waiting. To those of us who were born in "overdrive," waiting is not our favorite pastime. However, we discover that waiting on God in humility and faith because of who He is, and obeying His signals according to His timetable, are really where the exciting action is.
— Joy Dawson, *Intercession: Thrilling and Fulfilling*

How many of us rush around without knowing the secret of waiting on God? In order to move with His direction, we must learn this secret. How much time do we waste when we go down the wrong road? In waiting, we will live an overcoming life as we learn to walk in God's joy, peace, and contentment. When we wait, He will give us His secrets to kingdom living. By waiting for God's wisdom and direction, we will accomplish the most for Him.

Do we regard waiting as a burden? Perhaps. We should see it instead as the place of joy. When we wait, God tells us His secrets; He gives us our assignments. God wants us to walk in the Spirit, not in our fleshly nature. He is looking for those who can wait and let the flesh die so that the spirit can truly live for His purposes. Waiting on God in prayer brings forth His maximum purposes:

Find rest, O my soul, in God alone;
my hope comes from him. (Psalm 62:5)

In missionary circles, a story circulates about a missionary who was on a long trip through the African jungles with his African companions. They were traveling for several days on foot from one village to another, a considerable distance away. Several days into their journey, quite suddenly the Africans stopped and sat down. They set up camp for a few days, what seemed to the anxious missionary a great length of time. Not understanding why they were stopping, the goal-oriented missionary questioned his companions as to why the seemingly abrupt stop. The Africans smiled and said, "We are just stopping and waiting because we are giving time for our minds and hearts to catch up with our bodies."

For them it was a normal way of life. We can learn something from our African friends. Perhaps they have discovered the secret of true effectiveness. We often race through life without processing all that we are experiencing. We need to wait on God so our hearts can catch up with our actions.

In waiting, the very highest direction for your life can come forth daily. What may look like a loss of time is really only time multiplied on your behalf. God is able to do things with more efficiency than you are. The unnecessary falls away, and the very purposes and wisdom of God come forth in purity, holiness, and power. It isn't easy to integrate the discipline of waiting into your lifestyle, but when you embrace this, it will bring tremendous rewards. It should become a way of life to those who want to be used greatly by God. What are you waiting for today in prayer? Don't give up. It is in waiting that we make room for God.

Elisabeth Elliot, in her book *Keep a Quiet Heart*, says,

Waiting requires patience—a willingness calmly to accept what we have or have not, where we are or where we wish we were, whomever we live or work with. To want what we don't have is impatience and mistrust of God. Is He not in complete control of all circumstances, events, and conditions? If some are beyond His control, He is not God. A spirit of resistance cannot wait on God. . . . It is here and now that we must win our victories or suffer defeats. Spiritual victories are won in the quiet acceptance of ordinary events, which are God's "bright servants" standing all around it. Restlessness and impatience change nothing except our peace and joy. Peace does not dwell in outward things, but in the heart prepared to wait trustfully and quietly on Him who has all things safely in His hands. Can I not then wait patiently? He will show me the way.[1]

In John 11, the gospel writer recounts for us how Jesus delayed in responding to Mary and Martha when they sent word that Lazarus was sick. In fact, He stayed away a few more days, and Lazarus died. Time had run out. But Jesus' purpose in delay was to glorify the Father.

Have you been waiting for God to answer some of your prayers, and the answer has not come? The situation may look hopeless from every human standpoint, but God can resurrect any dream. He can break through even when we feel it is far too late. We fail to realize that God is using the time delay for our benefit—for maturing, for purifying the heart, for refining our character. He who sees the outcome wants to do a great work through us. The same resurrection power that brought Lazarus back from the dead is at work in our lives. The Lord wants you to look to only Him for your answer. Fix your eyes upon Him and wait, knowing He is faithful. God will come through for you in His timing. "Jesus said, 'Did I not tell you that if you believed, you would see the glory of God?'" (John 11:40).

Wait for the LORD; be strong and take heart and wait for the LORD.

— Psalm 27:14

LISTENING TO GOD — HEARING HIS VOICE

As you study your Bible, you may sense that God has something to say directly to you through the verses you are reading. Take a moment to consider the awesome reality that the God who spoke and created the universe is now speaking to you. If Jesus could speak and raise the dead, calm a storm, cast out demons, and heal the incurable, then what effect might a word from Him have upon your life?

— Henry and Richard Blackaby, *Experiencing God, Day-by-Day*

Listening to God and hearing His voice are awesome privileges and vitally important in intercession. It's so amazing that the God of the universe longs to speak to each one of us. Most of the people I know who are powerful prayer warriors have learned the art of being still before God and listening to Him. After all, good relationships always involve listening, not just speaking. One without the other doesn't work for long.

Hearing what someone is saying is extremely important to communication. Because we moved from country to country very quickly on our ship, we needed translators to help with the chronic communication barrier. We had numerous conferences and meetings in South America, and for the most important meetings, we had José, the very best translator on the ship. I remember a time when he was translating for a visiting American speaker. In the middle of his message, the speaker said, "What happened was so funny that it tickled me to death!" José turned to him and asked him to repeat himself. So he did. Again, José asked him to repeat himself slowly. The speaker said the same thing again. Finally, José turned to the audience and hesitantly said, "It was so funny that I scratched myself until I died!"

José had completely missed what the American speaker was trying to say. He was trying to listen carefully, but he didn't quite speak the language. Perhaps he needed more exposure to American idioms. Listening is important because we have to not only listen carefully to God but also understand what He is saying and what He means. The more we listen to Him, the more we learn to speak His language.

God loves to have us learn to listen to Him because He is always speaking and always has key things to say. In prayer we want to learn to wait in God's presence — to know the will of God for prayers that are on target. Being too busy is a big barrier to a strong prayer life. The world is noisy, and it takes time to hear God's voice. Let's look at some guidelines for stepping out of our noisy lives to hear God's voice:

Believe that God does speak to you. Accept this promise with expectancy. "My sheep listen to my voice; I know them, and they follow me" (John 10:27).

Find time to be alone with God. Take time to pray and listen. Yes, we are all busy, but being alone with God is of extreme importance if we are to hear clearly from Him. Often the Lord responds with a thought planted in our minds. It doesn't need to be something dramatic but may be like a still, small voice.

Test what you hear. Ask the Lord to confirm what you think He may be saying through the Holy Spirit so that you don't confuse His revelation with an Enemy thought. Check your motives.

Over time we learn to hear God's voice. "Dear friends, do not believe every spirit, but test the spirits to see whether they are from God, because many false prophets have gone out into the world" (1 John 4:1).

Examine everything carefully. Check all guidance with Scripture. What God is saying to you will agree with His Word. Second Timothy 2:15 says, "Do your best to present yourself to God as one approved, a workman who does not need to be ashamed and who correctly handles the word of truth."

Keep a journal of what God says. Journaling makes it easier to evaluate guidance. Try to journal on a regular basis.

Seek confirmation. Check with at least two other mature Christians before taking action. Be open to correction, especially from spiritual leaders.

Obey God. We must be willing to act on what God has told us. When we obey God, there is blessing. If we still doubt what we think God is saying, it is good to continue to ask Him for confirmation.

I find that taking time each day to sit in God's presence, listening to what He has to say, reading His Word, and journaling, enables me to pray more fervently and with greater authority. Learning to listen to God and hear His voice are key to a skillful prayer life.

The first stage of Moses' prayer training was wearing the noise of Egypt out of his ears so he could hear the quiet fine tones of God's voice. He who would become skillful in prayer must take a silence course in the University of Arabia. Then came the second stage. Forty years were followed by forty days, twice over, of listening to God's speaking voice up in the mount. Such an ear-course as that made a skilled famous intercessor.

— S. D. Gordon, "The Listening Side of Prayer"

SOAKING IN GOD'S PRESENCE

Jesus says, "Ask and you will receive." We're very good at the asking part but how about the "receiving"? If we are the ones who are doing all the talking, it's a pretty one-way conversation. Soaking is the listening part of our conversation with Him. It's laying aside time to lie down and receive from Him.

— Catch the Fire Ministries

The busyness of everyday life takes a huge amount of energy. Even a normal routine can be quite taxing. But why not add something to your schedule that will actually reenergize your life and lead you into a deeper dimension with God? If you integrate this into your life, it will be one of the greatest blessings you can possibly imagine. It's simple, and it doesn't cost anything except your time. And your time actually will increase as you learn to listen to God in this special way because you will eliminate unnecessary things from your schedule.

What am I talking about?

The blessing I am describing is called soaking in God's presence. The word *soak* means to drench, to wet thoroughly, to enter into the pores, and to be steeped in a fluid. Soaking in God's presence is drenching ourselves with God, being with Him, letting Him enter our entire life, and saturating ourselves with His presence through stillness, rest, and worship. A wonderful transformation occurs as we do this.

Those who practice soaking prayer find joy in their lives. It's a time to lay your burdens at the feet of Jesus. It's a time to find rest for your soul — to be still and know that He is God. It may take a little effort to quiet your racing thoughts, but it's well worth the effort. Let Him lead you beside still waters. Jesus says in Matthew 11:28-30,

> *Come to me, all you who are weary and burdened, and I will give you rest. Take my yoke upon you and learn from me, for I am gentle and humble in heart, and you will find rest for your souls. For my yoke is easy and my burden is light.*

So often we carry heavy burdens that God never intended for us to carry. God's burden is light. I have personally found that soaking in God's presence relaxes me more than anything else. It is where I have learned to exchange the heavy weight of everyday responsibilities for the joy and peace of God's strength. God is the one who makes me lie down in green pastures and leads me beside still waters. He is the one who restores my soul (see Psalm 23:2-3).

We all need to learn how to quiet our busy thoughts. God can help us turn our attention upon Him. Initially your thoughts can be racing all over, but know that the Lord is with you. Similar to the traditional practice of contemplative prayer, in soaking prayer you wait for your thoughts to settle. You come with nothing to do except sit or lie in God's presence. You are learning to focus on Jesus. When your mind wanders, you learn to bring it back. As you renew your mind and spirit, you will experience a greater peace. You will see things more clearly from God's perspective.

After soaking in God's presence, you will leave refreshed and full of the Holy Spirit. You will experience greater fruitfulness, and others will notice the difference. Your life will be transformed. You are learning a new dimension of walking in His Spirit. Instead of your striving to achieve things for God, He will be flowing through you. As a result, you will have an impact on the world around you; you'll carry God's presence with you wherever you go.

Begin by soaking in God's presence for at least twenty minutes. Do it daily, and watch what happens! In November of 2006, we had a monthlong 24/7 House of Prayer in southern Spain. Soaking prayer became a favorite for many individuals. It changed the lives of those who learned to soak in God's presence. Try it now through the personal application exercise that follows. I guarantee that soaking prayer will have a transforming effect on your life as well.

Soaking is a dedication: "God, this is time just for you." Soaking is an invitation: "God, do what you want to in me." Soaking is an expectation: "Thank you, Father, for what you are accomplishing as I rest in you." We come to Him like little children believing that He has good things for us. "If you then know how to give good gifts to your children, how much more will your Heavenly Father give the Holy Spirit to them that ask Him."
— Catch the Fire Ministries, www.ctfministries.com

PERSONAL APPLICATION

HOW TO SOAK IN GOD'S PRESENCE. Find a place without any distractions, put on some quiet music, get a journal or pen and paper, and get into a comfortable position. You may even want to lie on the floor. A peaceful environment helps you become peaceful on the inside.

- Listen to worship music. You may want to use quiet instrumental or vocal worship music. So much good soaking music is readily available (www.soaking.net is an excellent resource).
- Invite the Holy Spirit to come and soak you in His presence. Surrender your mind, body, and soul in prayer to the Holy Spirit. Humble yourself before Him. You are learning to wait upon Him.
- Focus on the Lord's presence. Open your heart to God. You are learning to abide in Him. You are learning to focus on Him and His presence. Wait for your thoughts to settle.
- Rest in faith and believe that God is working within you. It isn't about what you can accomplish through your efforts; it's about what God is doing in you. Write down any thoughts He may give you. Listen carefully to His voice.

- Give time to soaking in God's presence. The more time you can spend in His presence, the better. Start with twenty minutes. In a very short time, you will find that you want to spend more time in His presence.

HOW TO HELP OTHERS SOAK IN GOD'S PRESENCE. Get together with an individual or a group of people. Meet in a quiet place without distractions, and share the preceding list of directives before starting. Put on quiet worship music, have each person get into a comfortable position, and pray together "My Prayer to God" (which follows). Invite the Holy Spirit to come and soak each of you in His presence, and spend twenty minutes soaking in stillness before the Lord. Come together as a group and have a time of personal sharing of what the Lord was saying and what each person was experiencing and learning. Encourage each to make this a personal part of everyday life, and then close in prayer.

MY PRAYER TO GOD

Lord, teach me the secret of waiting upon You. Help me realize that this is key to effective prayer. Remove from my life anything unnecessary, and teach me to wait patiently before You. Quiet my active thoughts and help me soak in Your presence. I invite Your Holy Spirit to speak to me. I surrender my mind, body, and soul to You. Help me focus on You alone. Help me believe that You want to speak to me. Help me discipline myself to spend time in Your presence and be still on a daily basis. I want to know Your will by listening to You. Teach me to hear Your voice by examining everything carefully and keeping a prayer journal of what You are saying to me. I believe that as I soak in Your presence, Your life will flow through me to others. Thank You for teaching me to abide in You. I choose to be still and know that You are God [see Psalm 46:10]. I come before You with expectation. In Jesus' name, amen.

CHAPTER FIVE

THE INTERCESSOR AND THE BIBLE

Blessed is the man who does not walk in the counsel of the wicked or stand in the way of sinners or sit in the seat of mockers. But his delight is in the law of the LORD, and on his law he meditates day and night. He is like a tree planted by streams of water, which yields its fruit in season and whose leaf does not wither. Whatever he does prospers.
— Psalm 1:1-3

A LARGE BATTLESHIP sailed in the North Atlantic in blindingly dense fog. Suddenly the captain saw a light right in the middle of the ship's path. He immediately radioed the oncoming vessel, saying, "Alter your course ten degrees." Moments later a message came back, "Alter your course ten degrees." Knowing the seriousness of the situation, the captain became angry and again sent a message: "This is the captain. Alter your course ten degrees!" A reply quickly came: "This is a lighthouse. Alter your course ten degrees!"

The blinking light of a lighthouse is a welcome relief to every ship in a storm. A lighthouse does not change or move during turbulent weather. It is a lifesaver for sailors at sea when their ships can easily be thrown off course. It gives them a stable reference point, and they are then able to get to their destinations. I collect lighthouse models and photographs — they are all over my house. I appreciate what they stand for, and I always remember how important they were for us when we went out to sea.

In the same way, God guides us through the storms and uncertainty of life. Just as a lighthouse guides a ship, God guides us through His Word. The Bible is our fixed point that keeps us on course throughout life. The Bible helps us pray with greater power and accuracy. You may ask, *How can I learn to use the Bible in my prayers? How can I pray God's promises? How can I stay on course with God's Word?* Let's explore the benefits of praying the Bible and discover how to pray God's promises and meditate on Scripture daily.

PRAYING THE BIBLE

The life of a Christian is all about passion. Nothing is more powerful than when the Holy Spirit reveals the Son of God through the words of Scripture. Like the disciples on the road to Emmaus, every heart began to burn when God revealed Himself. When He unveils Himself and we have understanding of what He is saying, passion is the result.
— Wesley and Stacey Campbell, *Praying the Bible: The Pathway to Spirituality*

My Bible was worn out, so I simply prayed for a new one. I admit I was not actually expecting God to answer my prayer immediately. But the next day, someone handed me a new NIV Bible. What an exciting answer to prayer that was for a young missionary! I realized afresh that God is serious about His Word.

Everyone who is interested in developing a strong prayer life should pray the Scriptures during personal times with God. The Bible contains many types of prayers: the psalms, the prayers of wisdom, the Song of Songs, the prayers of the prophets, the prayers of Jesus, the apostolic prayers of Paul, and the hymns of Revelation. Additionally, God's promises run throughout Scripture. Praying the Word, along with worship, will have a dramatic effect on our prayer lives and prayer meetings.

The Benefits of Praying the Bible. Let's look at several important benefits of praying the Word of God:

- **You align yourself spiritually with God.** You begin to see things from a biblical standpoint and get a heavenly perspective of life instead of the world's system. "Set your minds on things above, not on earthly things" (Colossians 3:2).
- **You begin to pray things you have never prayed before.** Because you are praying the Bible, you pray with fresh strength from God. You can pray for the church with biblical apostolic prayers that are thorough and effective. For instance, "I pray also that the eyes of your heart may be enlightened in order that you may know the hope to which he has called you, the riches of his glorious inheritance in the saints" (Ephesians 1:18).
- **You receive authority from God.** Praying the Bible in the power of the Holy Spirit gives you a confidence and an authority because you are praying His truth, His will,

and His ways. You have more confidence in your prayers when you know that you are praying God's Word. "This is the confidence we have in approaching God: that if we ask anything according to his will, he hears us. And if we know that he hears us — whatever we ask — we know that we have what we asked of him" (1 John 5:14-15).

- **You defeat the works of the Enemy.** Praying the biblical directives defeats the Enemy because you are praying the very purposes of God. Satan is the father of lies, and when you pray the Bible, you pray God's truth. "'Is not my word like fire,' declares the LORD, 'and like a hammer that breaks a rock in pieces?'" (Jeremiah 23:29).

- **You are taken to a higher dimension in God.** You are led to places in God that you would never discover otherwise. His truth permeates your life dramatically. "As the heavens are higher than the earth, so are my ways higher than your ways and my thoughts than your thoughts" (Isaiah 55:9).

- **You become more passionate for God.** The Holy Spirit reveals the Son of God through the words of the Bible, creating a passion for Jesus. "Do not let your heart envy sinners, but always be zealous for the fear of the LORD" (Proverbs 23:17).

- **You learn the language of repentance.** Praying Psalm 51 alone will bring you into a deeper understanding of repentance. The Bible helps us express ourselves creatively and with deep reality. "Wash away all my iniquity and cleanse me from my sin" (Psalm 51:2).

In the last few years, I have gotten more involved in praying the Scriptures. I find it to be a great help to my prayer life. When I don't know what to pray, I go to the Bible. Using the Bible is a fantastic way to pray. Who can teach us better than God Himself? In our Sunday morning prayer meetings at church, we always pray the Scriptures. These times become powerful prayer meetings because God's Word gives us the best launching pad for all other prayers. The prayers seem to automatically take off from there. I also find that when I pray the Bible in other prayer meetings where doing so is an unfamiliar practice, it doesn't take long before others start to use their Bibles more in prayer. The Bible is powerful—we just don't fully realize the powerhouse it is. I want my prayers to originate from God because I know that those are the prayers that God certainly will answer. I believe that praying the Bible leads us into a deeper, more passionate prayer life.

Praying the Apostolic Prayers of Paul. Praying the apostolic prayers of Paul will powerfully enrich your prayer life. I have prayed them many times for the church worldwide and find them always fresh and alive. They move us to a new fervency of desire for the church's strength and for kingdom advancement. Paul, who had been persecuting the church, had a supernatural encounter with God that totally transformed his life. Having come face-to-face with the Lord, his prayers were anointed with the power of God. When we pray them, we flow in the same anointing.

In the apostolic prayers, Paul focuses on praying for the release of ministry gifts of the Holy Spirit and manifestations of fruitfulness, wisdom, and power. He yearns for godly character in the lives of the church. He prays that believers would know God better, that God would be glorified, and that His kingdom would come in the earth.

Paul prayed for:

- A spirit of wisdom to know God better (see Ephesians 1:17-19)
- Spiritual strength (see Ephesians 3:16-19)
- Abounding love in the church (see Philippians 1:9-11)
- Knowledge of God's will (see Colossians 1:9-12)
- Unity in the church (see Romans 15:5-7)
- Abounding hope (see Romans 15:13)
- Salvation of Israel (see Romans 10:1)
- Ministry that abounds in love and holiness (see 1 Thessalonians 3:9-13)
- Mature holiness (see 1 Thessalonians 5:23-24)
- Worthiness of God's calling (see 2 Thessalonians 1:11-12)
- Success of the gospel (see 2 Thessalonians 3:1-5)
- Open doors for evangelism (see Colossians 4:2-4)

Praying Paul's apostolic prayers definitely brings us to a new level in prayer and intercession for the church and the world around us.

Seeking the face of God, and then gazing at it, has to begin sometime and someplace. It begins by bringing our whole person before the consuming fire who is God, reciting His words — the Bible — out loud to Him and then letting the Holy Spirit reveal Christ to us. This is why we pray the Bible. May it be that as you engage in this practice that your prayer times will have the same result as the disciples — whose hearts burnt within as God talked with them along their journey of life. Yes, may your heart burn and your light shine.

— Wesley and Stacey Campbell, *Praying the Bible: The Pathway to Spirituality*

PRAYING GOD'S PROMISES

The Word of God is a great help in prayer. If it is lodged and written in our hearts, it will form an outflowing current of prayer, full and irresistible. Promises, stored in the heart, are to be the fuel from which prayer receives life and warmth.

— E. M. Bounds, *E. M. Bounds on Prayer*[1]

The Bible is filled with eternal truth and light for a lost, dark world. As we look around us, we see so many people who have no idea of the glorious light of Jesus Christ and the brightness of the gospel message. We have the outstanding and awesome privilege of proclaiming God's promises into the spiritual atmosphere over nations and cities. These proclamations of His Word will make an enormous impact, resulting in the fruit and harvest of God coming in due season. You may ask, "Can this really be true? Can we as God's praying people actually make such an unbelievable difference in this dark world?" The promises of God are "yes" and "amen" in Christ (see 2 Corinthians 1:20).

J. Hudson Taylor, the well-known missionary to China, is a great example of one who believed in the promises of God and demonstrated it through his life. In 1853, he was making his first voyage to China but was delayed because the winds had stopped. The rapid current was quickly sweeping the ship toward a reef. The sailors could not row the vessel away from the current, and it was becoming quite dangerous for everyone on board. The captain told Taylor that they had done everything they possibly could do. But Taylor told the captain that they hadn't prayed. He immediately told the three other believers on the ship to go to their cabins and pray for a breeze.

Taylor knew that God would answer their prayers for safety if they stood on His promises and prayed with confidence in God. He then went back on deck and asked the first officer to let down the sail because a breeze was on its way. The man refused but suddenly saw that the sail was beginning to stir. The breeze came, and they let down the sail and arrived safely at their destination.

God used Hudson Taylor in a mighty way in China through the mission he founded, the China Inland Mission. He was a man of faith in God and His Word. Once when he was going through an especially difficult time, he said to his wife, "We have twenty-five cents — and all the promises of God!"

The Word of God is a seed that grows. When God speaks His Word, He is sprinkling seeds that will bring forth His goodness and His purpose. The Word of God always produces, never returns void. Therefore, when you and I, guided by the Holy Spirit, speak God's Word into situations, we are sowing the promises of God, the immutable truth of God's Word. Then He will cause life everlasting to spring forth from those seeds.

Hudson Taylor stood on God's promises in faith, and God answered. Can we catch hold of something so powerful as this? It is time that we fill our intercession with the bold declaration of God's truth, expecting God's harvest.

So how do we pray the promises of God? How do we use what God says in His Word to pray for the world in which we minister and serve? Here are some practical suggestions for integrating scriptural promises into your prayer life:

- **Claim life verses.** What verses in Scripture are very meaningful to you personally? You may want to pray them daily. "I rejoice in your promise like one who finds great spoil" (Psalm 119:162).

- **Claim a promise for a specific situation.** God builds your faith when you pray certain promises over and over in difficult circumstances. "The LORD has kept the promise he made" (1 Kings 8:20).
- **Claim prayer promises as God brings them to mind.** Memorized Scripture really helps because the Word of God is planted in your heart, ready at all times for prayer. "The Lord is not slow in keeping his promise" (2 Peter 3:9).
- **Claim prayer promises as you read the Word of God.** Pray back to God the Scriptures that have impacted your spirit. This will change your life and situations. "Your promises have been thoroughly tested, and your servant loves them" (Psalm 119:140).
- **Speak God's Word into a situation.** Pray God's promises into your life circumstances. "My comfort in my suffering is this: Your promise preserves my life" (Psalm 119:50).
- **Speak and proclaim God's Word over your city or nation.** Doing this will have a powerful effect that will break the power of evil over the land, especially when there is corporate, united prayer. "Does he speak and then not act? Does he promise and not fulfill?" (Numbers 23:19).

"Is not my word like fire," declares the LORD, "and like a hammer that breaks a rock in pieces?"

— Jeremiah 23:29

MEDITATION AND PRAYER

What you think about in your unguarded moments reflects what your mind dwells upon. . . . The things you allow your mind to dwell on will be revealed by the way you live. If you focus on negative things, you will inevitably be a negative person. If you allow unholy thoughts to fill your mind, ungodliness will become common in your life. If you fill your mind with thoughts of Christ, you will become Christlike. What you fill your mind with is a matter of choice. Choose to concentrate on the magnificent truths of God, and they will create in you a noble character that brings glory to God.
— Henry and Richard Blackaby, *Experiencing God, Day-by-Day*

Learning to meditate on God's Word is essential for a powerful prayer life. Meditation guides us deeper with God, enabling us to pray on-target prayers and helping us to know more deeply His ways. Meditation is often a lost art because of the busy and noisy world in which we live.

Henry Ford once hired an efficiency expert to evaluate the Ford Motor Company. After a few weeks, the man gave a very good report, except for one thing. He complained about the man down the hall. The expert said that there was a man who was just sitting in an office with his feet up on a desk, appearing to be wasting his time. Henry Ford replied, "That man thought of an idea that saved us millions of dollars. And when he thought of it, he was doing exactly the same thing: sitting with his feet up on the desk!" That man was meditating (thinking and focusing his mind on one thing). It can look like a waste of time, but the best strategies for life will come when we take time to meditate on God's Word.

The secular world and even some cults are learning the importance of meditation. Several years ago, I worked on a team trying to reach the cults in Chicago. One of the popular cults in that city was rooted in transcendental meditation. Weekly the cult leaders had meetings open to the public, trying to entice everyone to come to their meetings. Our team went to a couple of their meetings and listened to them tell how much peace they had through meditating. Clearly, though, they were not meditating on God but using an empty mantra. We would pray fervently in those meetings for all the innocent visitors. Interestingly enough, on one occasion, just as the cult leader was talking about the peace he was getting through meditation, his chair collapsed right in front of everyone and he lost his peace! God answered our prayers that evening in an interesting way.

True meditation through God's Word is key to a life of spiritual fruitfulness. It keeps us from dwelling on the bad things we hear day after day in the newspaper and on the news. Meditation is different from reading, studying, or memorizing Scripture. It is the digestive faculty of the soul. It builds us up and refreshes and feeds our souls.

Biblical meditation involves taking a phrase, verse, or passage of Scripture and thinking carefully about it, pondering, and letting the Holy Spirit slowly make it alive within you. Meditation creates faith and expectation. Meditation focuses our thinking on God's Word. Through meditation we come to know God, not just about Him. Through meditation we grow in our love for God's Word. We read in Psalm 119:97, "Oh, how I love your law! I meditate on it all day long." Meditation helps us:

- **Get to know God.** This goes beyond just knowing *about* Him. We get to know Him personally as our King, our

Rock, our Redeemer, our Savior. "May the words of my mouth and the meditation of my heart be pleasing in your sight, O Lord, my Rock and my Redeemer" (Psalm 19:14).

- **Hear God's voice and keep from sin.** We are then able to pray on-target prayers. "I have hidden your word in my heart that I might not sin against you" (Psalm 119:11).

- **Change spiritually and gain insight.** We will always grow and God will change our hearts through meditation. "I have more insight than all my teachers, for I meditate on your statutes" (Psalm 119:99).

- **Walk in obedience.** It helps us to obey God and enables us to do the right thing in a moment that requires a sudden choice. "Be careful to obey all the law my servant Moses gave you; do not turn from it to the right or to the left, that you may be successful wherever you go" (Joshua 1:7).

- **Have something to share with others.** Often the very Scriptures that we meditate on are the ones someone else needs to hear and the ones we need to pray. "Within your temple, O God, we meditate on your unfailing love. Like your name, O God, your praise reaches to the ends of the earth" (Psalm 48:9-10).

- **Grow in a worshipping lifestyle.** As we ponder Scripture, we naturally grow deeper in our prayer life and are led more fully into worship. "I will meditate on all your works and consider all your mighty deeds. Your ways, O God, are holy" (Psalm 77:12-13).

- **Gain comfort and strength.** We gain spiritual strength when we meditate on Scripture. "Though rulers sit together and slander me, your servant will meditate on your decrees. Your statutes are my delight; they are my counselors" (Psalm 119:23-24).

- **Receive understanding and success.** God teaches us how to walk in success as we meditate on Scripture. "Do not let this Book of the Law depart from your mouth; meditate on it day and night, so that you may be careful to do everything written in it. Then you will be prosperous and successful" (Joshua 1:8).

Meditation helps us pray more effectively. Psalm 119 speaks over and over again about the value of God's Word and the importance of meditation. Meditating on the Scriptures will cause us to understand something of the mind and heart of God. It changes us deeply, freeing us from negative thinking because we are dwelling on the positive truth of Scripture. It touches the deepest part of our soul and transforms us. Meditation should always result in a response to God, whether it is repentance, thanksgiving, worship, obedience, or a change in attitude.

Whatever is true, whatever is noble, whatever is right, whatever is pure, whatever is lovely, whatever is admirable — if anything is excellent or praiseworthy — think about such things.

— Philippians 4:8

PERSONAL APPLICATION

HOW TO MEDITATE ON THE BIBLE AND PRAY GOD'S PROMISES. Get your pen and paper or journal, and get into a relaxing position. Start by slowly reading through Psalm 19. This is a psalm that my husband and I have memorized together. You may want to concentrate on a portion or the whole psalm. Then do the following:

- Let the Holy Spirit bring your attention to something in the passage. Maybe a certain portion of Scripture has really impacted you.
- Paraphrase the verse. Write it out in your own words.
- Make it personal. Relate it to your life situation.
- Try picturing what the verse is saying. Close your eyes and visualize it.
- Relate the verse or passage to other verses. Think about those other verses.
- Write something down. Write down any thoughts that have come to your mind and what God is teaching you through this Scripture.
- Respond. Think carefully about it and relate it to your life. How should it change your life? How will you practice this passage this week?

After your time of meditation, begin to pray these Scriptures back to God. Pray God's Word into your life situations. Speak and proclaim God's Word over your life, family, city, or nation. Pray about anything that God has shown you during your time of meditation, and respond in prayer to any direction He has given you. End by praying "My Prayer to God."

HOW TO HELP OTHERS MEDITATE AND PRAY GOD'S PROMISES. Read through this passage with a group or another individual. Ask God to speak to you. Take time to do the preceding meditation exercise, and then begin to share together with the group. Have someone write down the thoughts and ideas shared. Compare the different ideas. Then have a time of prayer applying it to your lives. Follow up with one another the following week and see how each person has applied the Scripture and what difference it made in each life. Pray "My Prayer to God."

MY PRAYER TO GOD

Lord, I pray that You would help me to use Your Word when I pray. Help me align myself spiritually with You by meditating on Your Word. Lead me and take me into a higher dimension than my own earthly thoughts [see Isaiah 55:9]. Help me think carefully about the verses I read, pondering on them and letting the Holy Spirit make them alive within me. Help me focus on Your Word. Teach me to pray Your promises over situations in my home, city, and nation. Teach me to establish things in the Spirit through Your Word. Give me faith to believe that when

I pray Your promise over a difficult situation, something happens in the spirit realm. You promise in Your Word that You fulfill Your promises and that Your Word is like a hammer that shatters the rock [see Numbers 23:19; Jeremiah 23:29]. In Jesus' name, amen.

CHAPTER SIX

THE INTERCESSOR AND PERSISTENCE

Jesus told his disciples a parable to show them that they should always pray and not give up.

— Luke 18:1

THE MINUTES WERE ticking away; the hour was late. We were somewhere in the middle of France with no idea where we were going. We had to face the fact that we were lost.

My husband and I needed to catch a ferry from France to England within a few minutes. We had been traveling for several days, and we were exhausted. In addition to that, we did not speak French, we had no French francs, and our vehicle was almost out of gas. Time was passing quickly, the gas stations were closed, and we had no clue what we should do.

You can imagine how difficult that night was! To be honest, our initial reaction was to grumble, but all of a sudden my husband thought of a better way to deal with this problem: He began to praise God right there in the car. He remembered Psalm 50:23:

He who sacrifices thank offerings honors me,
    and he prepares the way
    so that I may show him the salvation of God.

My husband chose to discipline his mind and think about God's Word and His promises. Together we laid this burden before the Lord in prayer. All the way to the ferry terminal, we persisted in prayer and praised God regardless of what would happen. In the end, we made it right to the line of cars waiting to leave for England, found a man with extra gas in a bottle, made it up the ramp to the ferry, and departed only seconds later.

Was this a miracle from God? I believe it was. When we practiced God's presence through praise and persistent prayer, God turned our circumstances around. Does God answer praise and persistent prayer in the middle of the night in a strange country? Yes, He does.

Discipline and persistence in prayer are not always easy. Sometimes we simply have to persevere, even when it looks the darkest. We ask, *How can I continue praying? Is there a way I can persevere in prayer even in difficult circumstances?* Let's explore how to keep on praying even when it's hard. We'll talk about burden-bearing intercession and how to carry God's heartfelt burdens in a proper way that can change our own circumstances and those of others.

PERSISTENT PRAYER

Persistent prayer is a mighty move of the soul toward God. It is a stirring of the deepest forces of the soul toward the throne of heavenly grace. It is the ability to hold on, press on, and wait. Restless desire, restful patience, and strength to hold on are all embraced in it. It is not an incident or a performance, but a passion of soul. It is not something half-needed, but a sheer necessity.

— E. M. Bounds, *E. M. Bounds on Prayer*[1]

Persistence is an important quality necessary for intercession for the needs of the world. Most of us have experienced praying for a long time for a specific prayer request and not yet seeing the answer. It takes faith to pray years and years for something. Don't give up! God continues to hear you. Persistent prayer carries a wrestling quality and an earnestness of soul. When you experience this, God is bringing you into a deeper level of intercession that is not through fleshly energy but by the Spirit of God. You will reap a harvest if you do not give up.

My mother prayed day after day for more than thirty years for my father's salvation. Many of us joined her in this prayer request, but we saw no indication on his part of even an interest in spiritual things. When he became very sick at age eighty, he easily could have died because of two major heart problems. We persisted in prayer for his spiritual and physical life. While he was in the hospital one night, he took the initiative and called us to come see him immediately. We hurried to his hospital room, not knowing what to expect. My mother led him in a prayer to receive Christ as his Savior. God used her to answer her own persistent prayer request! This was a huge reminder to all of us that God does answer prayer if we persevere.

If God can save my father after thirty years of prayer, I know that He can do anything. He wants each one of us to persist in prayer even when the answer seems impossible. We can take to heart Matthew 7:7-8: "Ask and it will be given to you; seek and you will find; knock and the door will be opened to you. For everyone who asks receives; he who seeks finds; and to him who knocks, the door will be opened."

The apostle Paul is a great example of persistent prayer. I am so amazed at his persevering prayer for the churches. He never gave up but kept on praying. Do we not also need to press on in prayer until the answers come? Paul prayed continually, earnestly, and unceasingly night and day for the churches, as shown in these verses:

- "Faithful in prayer" (Romans 12:12)
- "Night and day we pray most earnestly" (1 Thessalonians 3:10)
- "God . . . is my witness how constantly I remember you in my prayers at all times" (Romans 1:9-10)
- "Praying always for you" (Colossians 1:3, NASB)
- "I thank my God every time I remember you. In all my prayers for all of you, I always pray with joy" (Philippians 1:3-4)
- "For this reason, since the day we heard about you, we have not stopped praying for you" (Colossians 1:9)
- "With this in mind, we constantly pray for you" (2 Thessalonians 1:11)
- "I have not stopped giving thanks for you, remembering you in my prayers" (Ephesians 1:16)
- "I thank God . . . as night and day I constantly remember you in my prayers" (2 Timothy 1:3)

Paul did not give up; neither should we. Persistence will always pay off.

Another great leader knew the personal value of perseverance and persistence. When he was twenty-two years old, he failed in business. At age twenty-three, he ran for the state legislature and was defeated. He failed in another business at age twenty-four. He ran again for the state legislature and won. He had a nervous breakdown when he was twenty-seven. At age forty, he was elected to the U.S. House of Representatives, but two years later he lost for a second term. The next year, his three-year-old son died. At age forty-nine, he ran for the U.S. Congress — and lost. Did this man ever give up? Never. At age fifty-one he was elected president of the United States! His name was Abraham Lincoln. Although he knew so much defeat and loss in his life, because of his persevering attitude, he became one of the greatest men in history.

Maybe you have not yet seen the answer to your prayers for the salvation of your family members, the release of your ministry, or something else you are praying for. You may have been praying for a number of years and believe that God has led you in those prayers, but now you are tempted to give up. Do not listen to those thoughts. I urge you to continue in prayer. Do not faint, but be strong in hope and in faith. Continue, for God has a glorious result.

"Pray and never faint" is the motto Christ gives us for praying. It is the test of our faith, and the more severe the trial and the longer the waiting, the more glorious the results. The benefits and necessity of importunity are taught by the lives of the Old Testament saints. Praying men must be strong in hope and faith and prayer. They must know how to wait and to press, to wait on God and be in earnest in their approaches to Him.

— E. M. Bounds, *E. M. Bounds on Prayer*[2]

BURDEN-BEARING INTERCESSION

Intercession is not human beings prevailing on God, persuading Him to do something He does not want to do. It is exactly the other way around! Intercessory prayer is God finding someone on earth who will invite Him, in prayer, to do what He wants to do. He gives believers the joy and privilege of shaping the prayer in our own thoughts and words; but the more we practice prayer, the more artfully He will shape our thoughts until they are His, more and more cleanly.

— John Loren Sandford, *Healing the Nations*

Do you feel overwhelmed with so many needs around you? With all the people and situations needing prayer, we can easily feel overwhelmed. We need disciplined prayer lives, but how can we possibly pray for everything? How can we possibly handle the increasing pressure that is coming upon the world? And how can we enter into the place where we carry the burdens that God lays upon our hearts and live in joy and peace right in the midst of the battle? The Enemy will surely try to keep us unbalanced, pushing us to try to deal with the many needs around us. He will try to wear us out with anxiety. But God promises us that His burden is light and His yoke is easy (see Matthew 11:30).

The story goes that a young girl was miserable because of all the burdens she was carrying. One fall a heavy snowstorm arrived while the leaves were still on the trees. The girl's grandfather took her for a drive, showing her the trees heavy with snow. The branches on the elm trees were broken, but the pine trees were fine. He told her that there are two types of trees in the world: the foolish and the wise. An elm tree is rigid and quickly becomes weighed down with the burden of all that snow. Its limbs break under the weight. But the evergreen pine relaxes, lowers its branches, and lets the heavy weight of the snow drop right off. It remains unharmed. The girl's grandfather told her, "Be like a pine tree."

We also must be like the pine tree, giving our burdens to the Lord rather than trying to bear the weight of them ourselves. In the same way, when we pray for others, we are to bring the weight of each care to the Lord.

The Biblical Command. In Galatians 6:2, Paul commands us to bear one another's load. This command does not mean receiving someone else's pain or being overly burdened emotionally. We read in Isaiah 53:5,

> *He was pierced for our transgressions,*
> *he was crushed for our iniquities;*
> *the punishment that brought us peace was upon him,*
> *and by his wounds we are healed.*

Jesus is the One who carries the pain. He bears the burden. Mature intercessors release God's burdens in prayer rather than live under them. They take it to God and leave it with Him.

A woman told me that she knows so many Christians who bring their prayer requests to God, but a little while later are worrying about the same things. They are suddenly carrying the burdens again, letting them weigh them down with heavy concern. She shares this picture with them: Imagine getting a big platter. Put all your burdens and prayer concerns onto that platter as you pray. Then take the platter into your hands and throw it like a Frisbee up to God in heaven. Every time that concern comes and you begin to worry, remember that you prayed and gave it to God. Throw that platter of personal concerns back up to heaven. Remember that you gave it to Him and that God's burden is light.

Colabor with God. Burden-bearing prayer means working with God. Successful intercession begins in God's heart. The Holy Spirit takes the initiative and calls us into partnership with Himself as He acts. God stirs our hearts for the things that touch His heart. Sometimes we may sense the grief, hurt, pain, or anger of individuals or nations. The burden for people, cities, or countries can last for a single prayer, weeks, months, or even years. The battle to heal nations will call for great intercession and the burden for souls. God lays His burden upon our hearts, and we have the joy of praying it back to Him. He wants us to grow in His love and pray His burdens with joy, knowing that such prayers will dramatically change the world. How do we know which ones are from God, and how do we pray for them? The following and the personal application at the end of this chapter are adapted from the book *Beyond the Veil*, by Alice Smith:[3]

- **Have an attitude that accepts any burden God may want to give you.** God does not force you to bear a burden unwillingly. Be certain the burden is from the Lord, and you will be assured you are partnering with Him in victorious prayer.

- **Know that God will find someone to carry His burden.** When Queen Esther hesitated to bear the burden of her people on her young shoulders, her cousin Mordecai reminded her, "If you remain silent at this time, relief and deliverance for the Jews will arise from another place, but you and your father's family will perish. And who knows but that you have come to royal position for such a time as this?" (Esther 4:14).
- **Be aware of God's promptings.** God's promptings communicate His burden for intercession. You may sense a desire to weep or a heaviness in your spirit; a prompting by the Spirit can come in many ways: a quiet thought in your mind, a sense of emergency, a physical weakness, a dream, a mental picture of someone, or a deep longing to be alone with God and intercede.
- **As you begin to intercede, the prayer burden will intensify.** Accept this burden from God and give yourself to prayer.
- **Be aware of the Enemy's attacks.** Watch out for the Devil's accusations and attacks. Intercession should bring peace and joy when you finish. If the Enemy tries to bring condemnation, then submit to God and resist the Devil aloud (see James 4:7-8).
- **Believe God for victory.** He answers prayer in a powerful way. "The prayer of a righteous man is powerful and effective" (James 5:16).

When we enter into burden-bearing intercession, we can shed the fearfulness and anxiety of human emotions. We are better able to point people to Jesus and become examples to the lost and immature as we walk in deeper levels of rest in our Father's love, thereby bringing peace and healing to others. The world's confusion and chaos will cease because our prayers have touched the Enemy's strategies in a supernatural way. Satan's schemes will be thwarted and God's salvation can spring forth unhindered as we help ease the misery of humankind by praying prayers that come from the heart of God Himself. These are the goals of burden-bearing intercession.

Results of Burden-Bearing Intercession

- **You die to yourself faster.** When you carry God's burdens, you have to deal with sin issues in your own life. You experience death to self in a deeper way daily.
- **You love God more and grow in intimacy.** You share the heart of God and become more thankful to God as you bear burdens with Him.
- **Your Bible comes alive.** You identify with the hearts of biblical men and women as you gain greater understanding of how they carried the burdens of their time.
- **You experience personal repentance.** You learn to hate sin, because you see how much it cost Jesus. You repent as you learn to cry out to God for other people.
- **Your conscience becomes more sensitive to the Holy Spirit.** You are more aware of His conviction, whether in words or action.

Intercession is expressing a holy dissatisfaction with the way things are and taking the necessary steps to bring change through prayer. I envision a day will come when thousands of intercessors with militant, reckless abandonment for Jesus will stand up for the lost, stand against the powers of darkness and stand for the Kingdom of God. They will be radical.

— Alice Smith, *Beyond the Veil*

THE DILIGENCE OF PRAYER

Without persistence, prayers may go unanswered. Importunity is made up of the ability to hold on, to continue, to wait with unrelaxed and unrelaxable grasp, restless desire, and restful patience. Importunate prayer is not an incidental occurrence, but the main thing; not a performance, but a passion; not an option, but a necessity.

— E. M. Bounds, *E. M. Bounds on Prayer*

Prayer brings many joys, but we also must face the reality that prayer is hard work that takes discipline. After each victory in prayer, we must continue on. As I travel and go from one battle to another in prayer, I praise God for what He has done, taking time to be still in His presence and regain energy. An assignment from the Lord has been completed; we have seen the victory. I always realize that a new assignment is around the corner, and I need to be ready for the new challenge. Knowing that the flesh can never succeed against the Enemy, I rest in the Lord and listen as much as possible. This takes diligence. Then I am ready to enter into the new challenge in the wisdom and power of the Holy Spirit.

God seems to be moving in prayer worldwide. He is enlisting intercessors and raising the level of prayer power in many, many places. He is preparing us for things formerly beyond our grasp.

He has brought us to a higher place, and we must know we can go even higher. Prayer warriors are in tune with God's heart. They know the necessity of prayer and the urgency of the hour. I encourage you to passionately pursue God and His purposes in your life, family, church, and nation.

We can learn a lesson about diligence from a sixteen-year-old named William. Because his family was too poor to keep him, he left home with all his earthly possessions tied in a bundle. In his travels, William met an old man who was a captain of a canal boat. He told his life story to this man, mentioning that his only skill was in making candles and soap. The old man listened carefully, then prayed fervently for the boy. He said to him, "William, someone will be the leading soap maker in this city. Maybe it will be you. Give your life to Christ, be honest and good in all you do, give the Lord all that belongs to Him, and diligently make your soap and candles. God will prosper you!"

William considered the old man's advice and began to work hard and diligently. That young man was William Colgate, who prospered in business beyond his wildest dreams. He was able to give millions of dollars to the Lord's work because he listened to wise counsel and was diligent in working hard in order to make it happen.

We, too, must persevere in prayer. If we do, many things will happen spiritually. Through our prayers, we can spiritually give abundantly to the Lord's work. The value of prayer is like a rich treasure. Your prayers are more valuable than gold.

The following are several ways you and I can be diligent in prayer:

- **Stand your watch.** An intercessor is also a watchman, for a watchman's task is to be aware of any danger approaching the city. God places you as a watchman in prayer, being alert for potential Enemy attack. God is looking for intercessors to stand in the gap for entire cities and nations. What is the watch God has given you? Is it your workplace, home, neighborhood, or city? The psalmist exhorts us, "My eyes stay open through the watches of the night, that I may meditate on your promises. Hear my voice in accordance with your love" (Psalm 119:148-149).

- **Pray fervently.** Fervent prayer means that we spend enough time in prayer. We do not quit easily, but we cry out with our whole heart and soul. We may even pray with tears or groans that are too deep for words (see Romans 8:26). As James reminds us, "The [effectual fervent] prayer of a righteous man is powerful and effective" (James 5:16).

- **Pray steadfastly.** We must not be tempted by the distractions all around us. The life of Jesus is our example. He set His face resolutely to go to the cross. He was set to accomplish God's will. Faithfully labor with Him in this new dimension of holy resolve and steadfast prayer. The gospel writer recounts, "As the time approached for him to be taken up to heaven, Jesus resolutely set out for Jerusalem" (Luke 9:51).

- **Hold on to what is good in prayer.** We must diligently hold fast what is good and what has been won in prayer, for the Enemy will try to take it away. Satan hates what is good, and he comes to rob, steal, and destroy. He is after our victories. Hold fast to what we have won, even as we pray for further breakthroughs in intercession.

Prayer takes effort. To achieve something of great worth takes great effort. Prayer achieves a great purpose. A famous violinist named Fritz Kreisler said that as a violinist, he had to practice hour after hour, day after day for years. He had to always say no to other things. He had to miss going places and doing other things so that he could master the violin. The road was hard, but through diligence he became known as a famous musician. We, too, must practice prayer diligently, saying no to other distractions.

Do we ever get weary in prayer? Yes, we do. But I have personally seen that God's grace is sufficient. God will enable us to press through to higher ground, giving us the ability to be diligent and faithful as watchmen, strengthening us to hold on to what is gained in prayer. He will help us to persistently carry His burdens in prayer. God will give us Holy Spirit fervency and steadfast resolve in the battles that the body of Christ faces. How do I know this? I know this because I have tapped into a new level of His bountiful grace in my own life. So I challenge you to take hold of His wonderful empowerment, which is there for all of us. This requires discipline on our part, but remember the words of the apostle Paul in 2 Corinthians 12:9: "[The Lord] said to me, 'My grace is sufficient for you, for my power is made perfect in weakness.'"

Praying that influences God is said to be the outpouring of the fervent, effectual righteous man. It is prayer on fire. It does not have a feeble, flickering flame or a momentary flash, but shines with a vigorous, steady glow.

— E. M. Bounds, *E. M. Bounds on Prayer*[5]

PERSONAL
APPLICATION

HOW TO PRAY GOD'S BURDEN WITH PERSISTENCE. Take time to quiet your heart and mind before God. Have a pen and paper on hand for journaling. Begin praying in the following way:

- Go "fishing" to find out God's burden. Pray for those you normally pray for, such as your family members and friends. Then expand your prayers to include your community, city, or nation. When you feel God's tug on the line or a deeper passion arises, pray it through.
- Identify with God's desire. What does God want in this situation? Know that you are standing in the gap between God's desires and the Enemy's plans. Exercise your authority in Christ as you pray through the prayer burden. Ask God to stop the Devil's strategy. Thank Him for His victory in defeating the darkness.
- Intercede by faith for God's plans to be established. Ask God to show you how to establish His plans in prayer. Be persevering because God loves earnest, persistent faith.
- Stop when the burden lifts. You will know when the burden lifts or the breakthrough comes, as you will sense peace in your heart, your tears may cease, you may know the promptings of the Holy Spirit to stop, or the knowledge of victory may arise in your heart.

- Pray "My Prayer to God" (found at the end of this application). Pray it daily this week.

HOW TO HELP OTHERS PRAY GOD'S BURDEN WITH PERSISTENCE. Get together with a group or another individual for prayer. Welcome God into your presence, asking Him to lead and guide you in your prayers. Begin praying for a variety of topics, carefully listening to each prayer. Most often God will rest on a topic and several will feel a burden to pray regarding that topic. Don't move on to anything else until you have prayed through that prayer burden. After you are finished praying, discuss what you learned and what God taught you about burden-bearing prayer. End by praying "My Prayer to God" and ask God to continue to teach you about persistent, burden-bearing prayer individually during the week.

MY PRAYER TO GOD

Lord, I pray that You would teach me persistence in prayer. Help me to be like the apostle Paul, who constantly remembered to pray for others [see Romans 1:9-10] and did not stop giving thanks [see Ephesians 1:16]. Teach me to persevere even when I do not see the answer. Enlarge my faith and help me not to let go. I want to have an attitude that accepts the burdens You want to give me in prayer. Make me aware of Your promptings. Help me to believe You for victory. Enable me to be diligent in standing my watch in prayer [see Psalm 119:148]. Make me alert to Enemy attack in my family, city, and nation. I choose to move forward into a new dimension of holy resolve and steadfast prayer. Your grace is sufficient. I know that You will enable me to press through to higher ground as a watchman. Empower me in intercession. In Jesus' name, amen.

CHAPTER SEVEN

THE INTERCESSOR AND PURPOSE

O great and powerful God, whose name is the LORD Almighty, great are your purposes and mighty are your deeds. Your eyes are open to all the ways of men; you reward everyone according to his conduct and as his deeds deserve.
— Jeremiah 32:18-19

KING JEHOSHAPHAT WAS desperate: A vast army was coming against him. He resolved to seek the purposes of God. Instead of focusing on his problem and trying to figure things out on his own—what we often do—he looked straight to the Lord and said, "We do not know what to do, but our eyes are upon you" (2 Chronicles 20:12). When faced with an insurmountable challenge, Jehoshaphat responded by focusing on God's kingdom.

Jehoshaphat spent a lot of time praising God. He turned his eyes upon God first and praised Him for who He is and what He has promised. He praised God for His rulership over the kingdoms of the nations, for His power and might (see 2 Chronicles 20:6-9). Then he described the situation to God (verses 10-11). Finally he asked God to intervene and help (verse 12).

So often we reverse these priorities in prayer. We cry, complain, and advise God about what He should do. We spend very little time praising God for what He can do and consequently fail to see His plans and overall purposes. But the majority of Jehoshaphat's prayer was praising God, and the least amount was asking God to intervene. If we were in his sandals and had to consider the seriousness of this situation for ourselves, we would say that it was urgent and called for immediate action.

But Jehoshaphat's army was led by praise. They had discovered God's agenda in prayer. They faced the enemy singing. They had thanked God for the victory by faith even before seeing it. Second Chronicles 20:18 says, "Jehoshaphat bowed with his face to the ground, and all the people of Judah and Jerusalem fell down in worship before the LORD." The Lord set up ambushes against the enemy. And when the praising army arrived, the enemy was already dead. God had given them a tremendous victory. They returned joyfully and with great plunder because the Lord had given them cause to rejoice over their enemies (see 2 Chronicles 20:24-30).

Maybe you are facing a problem that seems overwhelming. You may ask, *How can I learn to focus on God instead of this huge problem? How can I be more purposeful in my prayer life?* In this chapter, let's learn to pray God's purposes and plans. We'll see how to eliminate distractions in our prayer life and discover God's agenda in prayer.

PURPOSE-DRIVEN PRAYER

God's divine purposes will be revealed to you as your heart touches His and begins to beat in rhythm with His. From this new level of relationship, you will move from problem-centered prayer to purpose-driven prayer. Problem-centered prayer is focused on our needs. Often we complain in prayer about a situation that needs a change. Purpose-driven prayer focuses on God's overarching plan. By faith you can pray for His maximum glory to be achieved in any situation. This frees the Lord to replace your problem with His provision!

— Alice Smith, *40 Days Beyond the Veil*

God wants to move us into a much higher realm of His will. We can get this revelation of His desires and plans only through intimacy with Him. As our hearts touch the heart of God, we have the same goals He has. His burden becomes our burden. We see things as He sees them, and we begin to understand His ways. We live in defeat when all we can think about is our own problems. We all have problems because we are not yet in heaven. It is time to enter into God's perspective to get the big picture and see God's heart. We become much more effective in prayer when we learn to study God's plans and pray His will. We read in Psalm 33:11,

> *The plans of the LORD stand firm forever,*
> *the purposes of his heart through all generations.*

Whatever your present problem is, God has a solution that is uniquely designed to fit your circumstances. He sees and solves problems perfectly, using His unlimited creativity. He can bring forth something out of nothing just as He created the world. Yes, even those things that seem to presently overwhelm you are no problem to Him. We try to explain things to God, but He already knows everything. We try to tell Him what we think the answers should be. However, God is omniscient and purposeful. He will answer our prayers in accordance with His will and purpose. Does this mean we don't pray about our problems? No, of course we pray about our personal concerns. But like Jehoshaphat, we concentrate on glorifying Him first. We seek the glory of His name (see Exodus 3:15; 9:16) and the establishment of His kingdom (see Psalm 145:13; Matthew 6:10; Habakkuk 2:14). As we take hold of this truth by faith, we move into a more effective level of prayer. Let's begin to move from our problems to God's solutions.

There are times in life when we cannot figure out what is happening to us. At times, I worry and become overly concerned with my problems. I have found that during such times, when I set my eyes on God and thank and praise Him right in the middle of difficult circumstances, things begin to change. Rather than rehearsing the problem over and over again in my mind, I am able to see how great and powerful God is. I notice that He works on my behalf when I choose to glorify His name. Philippians 2:13 says, "For it is God who works in you to will and to act according to his good purpose." My faith increases as I proclaim His works and choose to live for His kingdom purposes. I begin to see the big picture from His perspective, and as I do, I begin to live a more focused life.

We often don't realize that God has a solution to our every problem and is always watching, always caring for us. It's like a library that is so dark it seems closed. But the closer you get to the windows, the more you realize that there are people inside. The windows have dark film over them—you could see through it only one way. From the inside you could see everything outside. Our relationship with God is like this. He is always watching us. Frequently we act as though we are behind those reflective windows, thinking God doesn't notice us. We fail to realize that God sees everything—absolutely nothing escapes His eyes. His ears are attentive to our cries (see Psalm 34:15).

Let's remember that God sees everything and He cares. Let's see by faith beyond the horizon. Let's learn to focus on Him and His purposes.

For us to move from problem-centered praying to purpose-driven praying will require faith to look beyond our problems and see God's purposes. Faith removes mountains (Matthew 17:20). Faith sees beyond the horizon.
— Eddie and Alice Smith, *The Advocates*

A CALL TO FOCUSED LIVING

The biggest battle we each might fight is to stay focused on God long enough to learn how to abide in His presence. Before we can redeem the world, we must redeem our time. And we would think that with all the time saving conveniences we have in life, that this would be easy but it is not.
— Francis Frangipane, "Thy Face, Oh Lord, I Shall Seek"

God calls us to live a focused life, not a life scattered in many directions because of distractions. A focused life moves toward the center even in the busiest times because it is like a magnet attracted to Jesus, knowing that He alone is the One who makes everything work when priorities are in order.

Once while traveling throughout Europe over a four-month period of time, I faced the possibility of getting distracted by the many changes of culture and living conditions. We had been living in ship's cabins, rooms, houses, and hotels in different countries. We met all kinds of people from various walks of life. Because we were in one place for only a limited period of time, I desired to redeem that time by making the most of every opportunity to do God's will. I knew I couldn't do it myself, so I asked Him to help me keep focused on Him. It was a battle, I can assure you, but He answered my prayer. God is able to help each one of us live a focused life.

Even when we are settled in our own homes, everything seems to be rushing forward at the incredible pace characteristic of most of the world. So even then, I find the same necessity to ask God for a focused life. After battling through cancer, I have a greater passion to live a focused life. This is something every one of us needs to do, wherever we are in life, for we do not know what will happen tomorrow. Our prayer times with God must be guarded from distractions so we can focus fully on the plans and purposes He reveals to us. We must concentrate on God's best, remembering that prayer and abiding in His presence are of utmost importance. The Bible exhorts us in Ephesians 5:15-17, "Be very careful, then, how you live—not as unwise but as wise, making the most of every opportunity, because the days are evil. Therefore do not be foolish, but understand what the Lord's will is." The foolish person has no strategy for life and misses opportunities to live for God.

The famous golfer Arnold Palmer learned a lesson about focused living as a young man. It was the final hole of the 1961 Masters tournament. He had a one-stroke lead and had just hit a very good shot. A friend watching nearby leaned over the fence, reached out his hand, and said, "Congratulations!" Arnold took his hand and shook it proudly. In that short moment of time, he became overconfident and lost his focus. On his next two shots he hit the ball into the sand and then onto the green. He missed the putt and lost the game. He never forgot that mistake. In more than thirty years of golf since that time, he never again became distracted during a game.[1]

When you or I lose our focus, we can lose the game. We can miss our destiny and God's will for our lives.

Another compelling reason to stay focused on prayer is because it is easy to fall into sin. Most of us will not fall into sin suddenly. The Enemy takes us away from God in little ways, a slow erosion of our time with Him. Those who have fallen into sins such as immorality, pornography, or alcohol abuse often did not fall quickly; they slowly lost focus. Their time with God was replaced with worldly pursuits. Then, at the opportune time, Satan came suddenly with his temptation, and they were without the strength to resist him. The temptations in the world get stronger day by day. We must learn to focus on God in order to stand strong.

Make prayer and intercession a top priority in your life. Choose prayer as the first step and as your primary focus in your day. Having followed this pattern for years, I can vouch for the wisdom of seeking His plan and purposes. It has helped to order my life into His paths, bringing time-saving and stress-eliminating efficiency and keeping me from evil. It has also helped me to choose the best instead of just the good. Not only does Satan try to make a person fall into sin through stealing time with the Lord, but he also will try to keep you so distracted that you fail to do God's will in your life. Realize that prayer discovers God's agenda. Abiding in God and praying will make you a winner in all aspects of life.

Often, it is not evil pursuits that rob your time. Rather, the temptation is to sacrifice what is best for what is good. The enemy knows that blatantly tempting you with evil will be obvious, so he will lure you with distractions, leaving you no time to carry out God's will. He will tempt you to so fill your schedule with good things that you have no time for God's best. You may inadvertently substitute religious activity for God's will, pursuing your own goals for God's kingdom instead of waiting for His assignment. Time is a precious commodity. Be sure to invest it wisely.

— Henry and Richard Blackaby, *Experiencing God, Day-by-Day*

PRAYER DISCOVERS GOD'S AGENDA

Every time the Lord faced an important decision, He prayed. When He was being tempted to do things by the world's methods instead of the Father's, He prayed (Matthew 4). When it was time to choose His disciples, He prayed the entire night (Luke 6:12). If the Son of God required a night of prayer in order to determine the Father's mind, how long might it take us in prayer to clearly determine our Father's will?

— Henry and Richard Blackaby, *Experiencing God, Day-by-Day*

Let prayer set the agenda of your life. Many of us often worry about our lives: *What should we do next year? Where should we live? What school should we go to?* These are all good questions that need careful thought. But if most of us were honest, we would admit that we worry needlessly. It is right to get wise counsel and weigh out the options; however, when concern turns into unnecessary anxiety, we are not trusting God, who knows exactly how to handle every situation we face. Life becomes simpler when we seek God for every aspect of our plans. Our times spent in prayer will bring revelation of His agenda for us. We can be confident that in the final analysis, it is God who knows what is best for us and what will give Him the greatest glory.

Prioritizing prayer and letting Him set your agenda brings great peace. We lived for five years in Asia and experienced the typhoons that are so common in the Indian Ocean. Primarily they move in circles instead of from east to west or north to south. Before navigators understood their movement, they would try to maneuver out of the storm and often suffered serious destruction in the process. With a better understanding of typhoons, navigators have learned to locate the center of the storm—where it is totally calm—and go there. This is so much like prayer and discovering God's agenda. As we pray, we are able to circle in on God's agenda and find the center of His will. In this place, we experience His peace. When we try to get out of His will, we find destruction and chaos. Through prayer and renewing our mind in God's Word, we discover God's pleasing and perfect will (see Romans 12:2).

We must learn to pray about everything and trust in God's wisdom, which far surpasses ours. At times, we may sense His direction and feel the peace that comes from the Holy Spirit even though nothing may look logical according to our human perspective. I remember a time when my husband and I began to pray about lengthening our ministry time overseas because we felt God might want us to extend our visit to certain countries. We had already been traveling for two months, we were tired, we had much to do in the U.S., and my father was ill, so an extension needed prayerful consideration. There were other reasons why going home would have been the right choice from a human standpoint. The problem is, often God's viewpoint is different from ours. He sees things far in advance and from His perspective, which far surpasses ours.

Through prayer, we were circled in on God's agenda. We sensed His peace in staying longer, even though going home would have been easier and seemed more logical. In this case, we felt we had to go with the leading and peace of the Holy Spirit. The real key for us was prayer and waiting upon God, listening and hearing His voice.

We may not know the full picture of why we were to extend our time overseas, but we do know that we had to take that step of faith that was guided and empowered through prayer in order to do God's very best. We knew that we were in the right place and that when we did return home, we had completed what God had for us.

God loves to hear us pray with fervency and then listen and step out in faith according to His leading. Perhaps there is something you need to pray over regarding God's plan and purpose in your present circumstances. Praying through every decision, listening to His voice, and leaning upon His wisdom will enable you to determine His agenda. Proverbs 3:5-6 says,

> *Trust in the LORD with all your heart and lean not on your own understanding;*
> > *in all your ways acknowledge him, and he will make your paths straight.*

How can we hear God when we pray? Here are some guidelines to help you hear His voice as you seek Him in prayer:

- **Bathe your life in prayer.** Pray about all the decisions in your life daily. Ask Him for direction so that you may fulfill His will for your life for that day. Continually bring major decisions to Him in prayer. Pray, listen, and wait with expectancy.
- **Believe that God does speak to you.** Accept the promise in John 10:27, "My sheep listen to my voice; I know them, and they follow me."
- **Find time to be alone with God.** Take time to pray and listen. Most of life is very busy, but time with God is of utmost importance so we can hear from Him. Often the Lord responds with a thought planted by His Spirit into the mind or heart.
- **Keep a journal of what God says.** We can better evaluate guidance and see what God is saying when we journal on a regular basis. Journaling helps us ponder our thoughts and impressions so we can clearly discern the path God wants us to take.
- **Test what you hear.** What we think is God's voice may come from the Holy Spirit, the Enemy, or our own souls. Ask the Lord to confirm what you think He may be saying. First John 4:1 exhorts us to test the spirits. It's good to seek confirmation from at least two other Christians before taking action, especially on big decisions.
- **Carefully check all guidance with Scripture.** God's Word is truth. What we think God is speaking should

line up with Scripture. This is why we should examine everything carefully with the Bible.

- **Obey God.** We must be willing to act on what God has told us. When we obey God, there is blessing. If we still doubt what we think God is saying, it is good to continue to ask Him for confirmation until we sense His peace.

Let's follow these guidelines and practice listening to God. Let's learn to eliminate the distractions in our life.

Jesus knew that His mission was not to attract a crowd, but to remain obedient to His Father. It was prayer that set the agenda for Jesus' ministry (Luke 6:12). Prayer preceded the miracles (John 11:42-43); prayer brought Him encouragement at critical moments (Luke 9:28-31); prayer enabled Him to go to the cross (Luke 22:41-42); and prayer kept Him there despite excruciating pain (Luke 23:46). Follow the Savior's example, and let your time alone with God, in prayer, set the agenda for your life.
— Henry and Richard Blackaby, *Experiencing God, Day-by-Day*

PERSONAL APPLICATION

HOW TO LIVE A FOCUSED AND PURPOSEFUL LIFE. Begin by spending time in praise and worshipping God. Then meditate on some of the following Scriptures: 2 Chronicles 20:6-12; Jeremiah 32:18-19; Psalm 33:11; 145:13; Exodus 3:15; 9:16; Matthew 6:10; Habakkuk 2:14; Philippians 2:13; Ephesians 5:15-17; Romans 12:2; Proverbs 3:5-6; Micah 7:7; and Luke 6:12. Spend some time in prayer and waiting upon God. Then carefully answer these questions, which are designed to help you eliminate distractions in your life:

- What are some ways the Enemy is distracting me, causing me to waste my time?
- What good things in my schedule are leaving no time for the best? What can I eliminate?
- What is the order of priorities in God's plan for me?
- Am I keeping prayer as a top priority in my life? In what way can I improve?
- Am I keeping God as my main focus? How am I abiding in Him, and what is keeping me too busy?
- How am I purpose-driven in my prayer life instead of problem-centered?

Review this list, and write a prayer to God telling Him what you will do about ordering your priorities this week. Put your prayer into practice. At the end of each day, read through these questions and evaluate your day and whether you are living a focused and purposeful life. End each day with "My Prayer to God" (found at the end of this application).

HOW TO HELP OTHERS LIVE A PURPOSEFUL LIFE. Get together with another individual or group, and ask God to speak to your hearts. Spend time in worship and praise, then read through some of the passages presented in this chapter. Give each person paper and a pen, and individually answer the above questions. Give adequate time (twenty to thirty minutes) so that everybody can carefully think through these questions as well as the Scriptures. Then come together in a group and share your answers. This should lead to an in-depth, honest discussion. Conclude with a time of prayer either spontaneously as a group or by having each person pray for the person on his or her right. End your prayer time by praying "My Prayer to God."

MY PRAYER TO GOD

Lord, enlarge my vision. Help me get in tune with Your purposes and understand Your ways. Help me move into a more effective prayer life. I pray that You will bring creative solutions to the problems I face. I choose to be purpose-driven rather than problem-centered. I choose to pray according to Your purposes. Help me see with my spiritual eyes of faith. Help me commit myself to Your glory rather than to my own success. Help me see beyond the horizon. Eliminate the unnecessary from my life and help me live a focused life. Order my priorities and enable me to prioritize prayer. Set the agenda for my life, and teach me to hear Your voice. I believe that You want to speak to me. I thank You that I can bring glory to Your name and establish Your kingdom through my prayers. In Jesus' name, amen.

CHAPTER EIGHT

THE INTERCESSOR AND STRONGHOLDS

The LORD is my rock, my fortress and my deliverer; my God is my rock, in whom I take refuge. He is my shield and the horn of my salvation, my stronghold.
— Psalm 18:2

WHEN A FEW people on board the *Doulos* began feeling ill, it wasn't a major problem. We had a doctor on board who took care of the crew. Situated in a tiny doctor's cabin with two nurses and another small hospital cabin, the doctor easily could handle a few sick individuals. During my years sailing from nation to nation bringing the good news of Jesus, we would face many battles of great intensity. Amazingly enough, with an international crew of such diverse backgrounds, God seemed to keep illness at a minimum.

The ship had just left Papua New Guinea — a beautiful, lush, jungle-like land, but one infested with malaria. The sick individuals were quickly diagnosed as having malaria and were sent to bed immediately. A few days passed, and a few more of the ship's crew felt sick. They, too, were checked for malaria. Sure enough, they had it! Suddenly more and more people were diagnosed with malaria.

People felt sicker by the day. Soon malaria became the main topic around the meal tables. After breakfast, we had daily morning devotions together on the ship. Each day a graph was put up that showed how many people had malaria. It was growing at an alarming rate. The whole ship became consumed with thinking about illness. It affected not only the ministry but our personal lives as well.

Finally a physician who was also a counselor came on board. He was astounded at what was happening. He firmly reported that we were all looking inwardly at ourselves and that we had believed a big lie. We couldn't possibly all have malaria. A group of medical students from South Korea arrived and tested everyone with their microscopes. In actuality, only two or three people had malaria. It turned out that the ship's microscope was old and dirty. What had looked like malaria was simply little pieces of dirt on the microscope. We were all deceived—even to the point of actually feeling sick. What the entire ship's crew had believed was a lie and not the truth!

In the same way, Satan attacks us with his form of strongholds—deceptive lies that come in through our thoughts and take root in our lives. They seem true because we have believed them most of our lives, but they are like the dirty microscope. They are not showing us the true picture. The warfare that you and I are involved in is not a fleshly war, and neither are our weapons. It is a supernatural war and a spiritual warfare that centers within our thought life.

You might ask, *What lies am I believing that have affected my life? What have these lies done to my prayer life? How do I destroy these strongholds and walk in God's truth?* Let's open up the arsenal and find the weapons to destroy strongholds in our minds. Let's learn how to make God and His Word our stronghold, choosing life on a daily basis.

DESTROYING PERSONAL STRONGHOLDS

Though we live in the world, we do not wage war as the world does. The weapons we fight with are not the weapons of the world. On the contrary, they have divine power to demolish strongholds. We demolish arguments and every pretension that sets itself up against the knowledge of God, and we take captive every thought to make it obedient to Christ.

— 2 Corinthians 10:3-5

As we develop in our walk with God, the Enemy will fight hard to discourage and defeat us. To overcome these personal attacks, we must understand his methods. A primary method is trying to defeat us through our thought lives. This battle is fierce because it goes on continually. In dreams, when we wake up in the morning, and throughout the day, fiery thought darts assail our minds. Our Enemy knows that if he can rule in our thoughts, then he can defeat us in our actions, including our prayer lives. We don't realize the number of negative thoughts that bombard us daily. And they are powerful. They can destroy relationships, affect ministries, and drain us of health and energy.

These destructive thoughts are called strongholds because they can take such a paralyzing grip or "strong hold" on us. Learning to destroy strongholds of the mind will have a dramatic effect on the life of the person who wants to serve God wholeheartedly. To avoid destruction, we must learn to take every thought captive to Christ and not listen to the lies of the Enemy. Doing this has greatly impacted my life. Having gained an understanding of how to walk free of strongholds, my husband and I have been able to teach people how they, too, can walk in a greater freedom. This has been one of our main teachings resulting in life-transforming results because we find this to be a major problem everywhere we go. If the Devil can get to you in your thinking, he can defeat you. The battlefield is in the mind.

A Powerful Enemy—Strongholds of the Mind. The Enemy's stronghold is a thought pattern that may even be planted in our minds during our first years. It grows and gains strength throughout the years, becoming a practiced way of thinking and an automatic way of living. We all have some strongholds that have become powerful life messages. Psalm 18:2 and many other verses remind us that God is our true stronghold, the strength we cling to. But in our ordinary living, it's easy for Satan to present us with substitute strongholds and watch us cling to the wrong thing.

An Enemy stronghold is based in a lying thought that we have embraced in the place of God's truth. These strongholds are powerful and can cause destructive habits that affect our relationship with God and with others. Such patterns of thought can bring terrible misunderstandings into our lives. Read these examples of strongholds, and imagine what life would be like for the person who believes one of them:

- "I will never change."
- "I'm bad."
- "Nobody loves me."
- "I'm stupid."

- "I'm a failure."
- "It's all my fault."
- "Life isn't safe."
- "My situation is hopeless."

These thoughts become open doors through which the Enemy can defeat us again and again. We are then stuck in a rut. Picture a truck driving down an old worn-out road filled with deep ruts all along its path. It's hard to drive outside the grooves. The truck automatically follows the path of the ruts.

Carol was a worship leader in the north of Wales, but nobody was asking her to lead. She felt rejected. She was part of a church that had in previous years experienced degrees of revival. We met with Carol one evening as she angrily told us her situation. At one point we asked her, "What is the Devil saying to you?" She replied, "Nobody wants me." She was facing the stronghold of rejection. It actually had haunted her most of her life, but she just couldn't see it. The lie was embedded in her mind and heart since early childhood. It had become a deep groove in her life, and she had lived it out on a daily basis, carrying it with her all these years. The stronghold affected her life, ministry, and relationships everywhere.

When we asked her if God had said this, her response was, "No." The first attempt to lead her in prayer failed. Her anger with the Lord was great. The Holy Spirit inspired my husband with a picture, and he asked, "Carol, if the Lord gave you a scepter and said that if you raised it, you would bring revival to all of Wales, would you raise it?" She said, "Yes!" My husband then said, "The Lord has given you a scepter and by raising it, you will bring revival to your own life." Then with tears she repented of the lie, and God broke through! Finally the lights went on, and she was able to see that it was a lie after all! This is the joy of breaking strongholds. To suddenly see the lie for what it is — a path of destruction — is an incredible discovery.

The following week, several positive things came her way quite unexpectedly. Someone encouraged her with a verse. A main leader in her church suddenly asked her to lead worship. Other blessings came her way. Why the dramatic change? Sometimes the Lord will hold us back from using our gifts because He wants to get at something deeper in our lives. Carol broke that stronghold, and blessings — previously hindered — were able to come her way.

Our strongholds affect one another, which is why there is so much warfare in marriages and relationships. They trigger one another's emotions or strongholds and work to bring destruction. We need to bring them to the Cross in repentance. First John 3:8 says, "The reason the Son of God appeared was to destroy the devil's work." We need to believe that Jesus' death on the cross has set us free. If we begin to walk out of these strongholds and believe the truth instead of the lie, Satan knows we will be unstoppable for the kingdom of God. That is why he fights so hard to keep these lies hidden in our lives. But there is hope! God can identify and break these strongholds in our minds.

Weapons Against Strongholds. Taking every thought captive to the obedience of Christ is not necessarily an easy thing to do — this is spiritual warfare, after all. Here are some weapons to help us to deal with misguiding strongholds in our own lives and the lives of others:

- **The Word of God.** The Word is our life and sets us free. We must hold on to it with all our hearts. We must listen to what God says rather than the lies and fiery darts of the Enemy.

- **Repentance.** Repentance removes the legal base of Satan's attack. When we confess the false belief that we have carried most of our lives, God is able to remove the legal base and close the door on the Enemy. He is able to break through the fear that has controlled us. He can speak to our hearts in a new way so that we are able to experience His peace and love in a new dimension.
- **Personal testimony.** We overcome the Enemy by the word of our testimony. Personal testimony touches into the feeling part of our being. When given in a spirit of humility, it brings encouragement and helps us identify with another person. As John reminds us, "They overcame him by the blood of the Lamb and by the word of their testimony" (Revelation 12:11).
- **Forgiveness.** We must forgive everyone who has hurt or offended us. Usually when strongholds are detected and acknowledged, there is someone who has been involved in starting or reinforcing that stronghold. Forgiveness will be a key to our deliverance. In the next chapter, we will learn about forgiveness and how to set those people free.
- **The blood of Jesus.** There is power in the blood of Jesus. This is power to set the captives free and live a new kind of life. The blood of Jesus overcomes all obstacles of sin. We need to learn to pray the blood of Jesus over our cities, our neighborhoods, our families, and our own lives.
- **Prayer.** Prayer applies to the blood, cross, and resurrection life of Jesus. It enables us to hear and receive the Word of

God. We read in Ephesians 6:18, "Pray in the Spirit on all occasions with all kinds of prayers and requests. With this in mind, be alert and always keep on praying for all the saints."

- **Dying to sin.** We need to hate the strongholds in our lives and our sinful responses. We need to be so grieved by our sinful strongholds that we are willing to pay the price of dying to sin. It is a process. Paul exhorts us, "Love must be sincere. Hate what is evil; cling to what is good" (Romans 12:9).

God will enable us to break through the Enemy strongholds in our lives. We can be transformed by the renewing of our mind. Let us not give up but diligently bring our thoughts captive to the obedience of Christ. We must learn to make God our stronghold.

I urge you, brothers, in view of God's mercy, to offer your bodies as living sacrifices, holy and pleasing to God — this is your spiritual act of worship. Do not conform any longer to the pattern of this world, but be transformed by the renewing of your mind. Then you will be able to test and approve what God's will is — his good, pleasing and perfect will.

— Romans 12:1-2

GOD IS MY STRONGHOLD

Thinking about what you're thinking about is very valuable because Satan usually deceives people into thinking that the source of their misery or trouble is something other than what it really is. He wants them to think they are unhappy due to what is going on around them (their circumstances), but the misery is actually due to what is going on inside them (their thoughts).

— Joyce Meyer, *Battlefield of the Mind*

Our victory will come as we face the negative strongholds in our lives and learn to stand in God's Word. Enemy strongholds bring serious devastation into our lives. They hinder our victorious stance in prayer by keeping us preoccupied with negative thinking. The Devil has a strategy for his warfare, a well-laid-out plan of deliberate deception. He hates prayer and will do anything to stop us from praying, but Christ has brought the victory by the word of His power in truth and love.

How can we face and break free of Enemy strongholds? How do we overcome these defeating thoughts? Always remember this: Our minds are the battlefield. How can we have God's Spirit flow through our lives unhindered by this negative and destructive thinking? The problems we are dealing with here are internal thoughts and attitudes. Satan knows that by controlling our thoughts, he can influence our actions. Let us look at ways to face and overcome the Enemy strongholds in our lives:

- **Realize that you cannot destroy personal strongholds by yourself.** The battle is in the spirit realm. God's divine power will demolish strongholds. You can't overcome strongholds by determination alone. Only God can do it. We often try to take surface thoughts captive, not knowing the root thoughts from which the surface ones spring. Paul says clearly, "Though we live in the world, we do not wage war as the world does. The weapons we fight with are not the weapons of the world. On the contrary, they have divine power to demolish strongholds" (2 Corinthians 10:3-4). It's as simple as praying, "Lord, I realize that I cannot destroy the strongholds in my life by myself. I acknowledge my dependence on You to do it."

- **Ask God to deal with the strongholds in your life.** He is the only one who can demolish the strongholds, fortresses, vain imaginations, arguments, and erroneous ideas. Our flesh doesn't want to see our strongholds go. Our flesh wants to live the old way. We need to invite God to show us the strongholds and motivations of our hearts.

> *Search me, O God, and know my heart;*
>   *test me and know my anxious thoughts.*
> *See if there is any offensive way in me,*
>   *and lead me in the way everlasting. (Psalm*
>   *139:23-24)*

Pray, "Lord, I resolve to deal with the strongholds in my life. I ask You to get to the roots. I ask You to show me the motivations of my heart and my hurtful ways. I invite You into the center of my life to reveal to me the lies I have believed."

- **Be aware of your thoughts.** Is your self-talk like this? "I'm no good." "I'm a failure." "I never can do anything right." "Life is hopeless." Although these are simple thoughts, they indicate strongholds. Be aware of sudden negative emotions, as they point out that you are touching a stronghold. By watching your thoughts and looking for false mindsets, you are able to see them more clearly. In both of his letters, the apostle Peter desires to stimulate his readers to positive and wholesome thinking. In 2 Peter 3:1 he says, "Dear friends, this is now my second letter to you. I have written both of them as reminders to stimulate you to wholesome thinking." As you practice paying attention to your thoughts and looking for false mindsets, you are able to see them more clearly. Pray, "Lord, make me aware of my thoughts. Show me my strongholds and negative thought patterns in my life. Help me recognize these patterns very quickly. Open my eyes to see the lies I have been believing and the truth of Your Word."

- **Be patient and persistent.** It took you a lifetime to reinforce these strongholds, these negative thought patterns. They are like grooves in your life. It takes time and effort to be free of them. We often want a quick fix. The quickest fix is if you determine to deal with them on a daily basis. Don't give up, but face them every time you start feeling down. Paul wrote to the Galatians, "Let us not become weary in doing good, for at the proper time we will reap a harvest if we do not give up" (Galatians 6:9). Pray, "Lord, give me endurance and patience to walk free of these negative thought patterns. I know that it is not a quick fix. I accept Your timetable in dealing with these strongholds. I choose to be persistent in dealing with them."

Johannes wasn't able to sleep. A missionary in southern Spain, he was at a local university studying when one of his professors caused him offense. In anger he mulled over the incident, even influenced the other students against the professor. Anger resulting in sleeplessness was taking hold of him. Johannes came to our seminar on breaking strongholds. He told us that every night he would take his professor to bed with him as he bitterly thought about him over and over again. We asked him to list the thoughts that were resulting from the situation. Being German, his list was short on emotions and words. It was something like this: "I am small and he is big." It was a David-and-Goliath situation, but this David didn't have the faith of the other. Johannes believed that he was insignificant. We asked him, "Did God say this?" He said, "No!" Johannes suddenly became aware of his negative thought pattern. We prayed with him, and he broke the stronghold in a serious and down-to-earth manner. He confessed his offense against God in a very matter-of-fact way, and God heard.

Everything changed dramatically. That night, Johannes slept well. The next day, he was so changed that he had the opportunity to share Christ with the class in a deeper way than ever before. Johannes still has to guard his thought life and break the strongholds as the fiery darts come. He must be aware of his thoughts and determine daily to deal with the strongholds, but he can walk in new victory as he walks in God's truth. Breaking spiritual strongholds can change your life too. If you practice the truth in this chapter, you can have a changed life. Each of us has the opportunity to choose life daily.

Praise be to the LORD my Rock, who trains my hands for war, my fingers for battle. He is my loving God and my fortress, my stronghold and my deliverer, my shield, in whom I take refuge, who subdues peoples under me.

— Psalm 144:1-2

CHOOSE LIFE

This day I call heaven and earth as witnesses against you that I have set before you life and death, blessings and curses. Now choose life.
— Deuteronomy 30:19

Every day when we get up, we make a multitude of choices. The most important choice you or I can make in the details of everyday life is whether we will choose life or death. Will I choose to believe God's Word or a lie? Will I choose God's way of life — peace, God's thoughts, obedience, and walking in His Spirit — or will I choose death — my own way of living and thinking, my own will, and walking in the flesh? We need to be careful to always walk in God's Spirit and not give in to our own fleshly tendencies. Choosing life makes a big difference in our prayer lives. We read in James 5:16, "The prayer of a righteous man is powerful and effective." Righteous thinking and living results in a powerful and effective prayer life. It is choosing to go God's way with God's thoughts about us instead of going the way of death and believing the lies of the Enemy. It is holding on to God's Word and obeying Him moment by moment in every detail.

We need God's Spirit to help us choose life, and we need divine power to deal with strongholds in our lives. Emotions won't change overnight; our thoughts can be destructive and pull us down. God wants us to think His thoughts. We must cast out these negative thought patterns and take God's truth into our innermost being for the rest of our lives. God is truth, and Satan is the father of lies. His aim is to defeat us, and he attacks us through nagging thoughts, doubts, fears, and reasoning. If the Enemy can control our thoughts, he can control our actions.

What are some ways we can have victory over these destructive strongholds? How can we choose life and begin to walk free?

- **Look for a very real encounter with the Lord.** What are some verses God has used to speak to you deeply? Spend time in His presence. Pray for God to show you how He thinks about you. Pray, "Lord, You have spoken to me so deeply in this verse [read the verse]. Thank You for Your love for me and for Your truth. Please speak to me."
- **Replace the lies with the truth of His Word.** Study God's Word daily, and hide it in your heart. Pray, "Lord, I want You as my stronghold. I never want to believe these lies about myself again. I choose to believe Your truth."
- **Ask the Lord for new emotional responses to the lies of the Enemy.** Pray for emotions that correspond with God's truth. Pray, "Lord, I want new emotions. I pray that You exchange my [name negative emotions] with Your peace, Your contentment, and Your joy."
- **Expect to walk in new godly motivations and reactions.** When God becomes your stronghold, Jesus is your source. Your motivations change. Pray, "Lord, I choose to walk in Your Spirit. I choose to react Your way. I choose to lovingly react to others. Change me, and make me like You."
- **Daily decide to choose life.** The victory over our thought lives is a daily battle. Pray, "Lord, today I choose life. I choose Your ways. I choose to obey You. I choose not to listen to the Enemy's lies."

As I look back on my years on the mission field, I realize that learning how to break personal strongholds and walk in God's truth has been one of the most important things I have discovered in my life. So often I was battling Enemy attacks without knowing how to thoroughly deal with the strongholds. I had believed lies and didn't even know it. One stronghold in my life was the belief that life wasn't safe. I traveled all over the world on a ship. Imagine the excess stress and energy I was using because of that stronghold. Life at sea is full of turbulence, and I felt anxious. Since breaking that stronghold several years ago, I am much more at ease, and I can relax in ways I never knew before. I know that God is in control and I can trust Him.

I would encourage you to go over these truths about breaking strongholds again and again. It takes time to take them deeply into your life and thoroughly apply them, but it makes so much difference. So many believers struggle simply because they believe a childhood lie that has devastated their victory. Know that Jesus wants to give you an abundant life free of negative thinking. We no longer need to listen to the lies of the Enemy. Jesus Christ is our strong tower. Bring your false beliefs to the Cross, and watch Him bring you to a new level of freedom.

The thief comes only to steal and kill and destroy; I have come that they may have life, and have it to the full.

— John 10:10

PERSONAL APPLICATION

HOW TO BREAK PERSONAL STRONGHOLDS. When something is bothering you and when you notice harmful, recurring patterns in your life, you must look at what you believe, what you are feeling, and how you are behaving. You will need time for this exercise, but it will be well worth it. Get out a piece of paper and make three columns. Label the columns "Thoughts," "Emotions," and "Behaviors." Then do the following:

- Ask God to reveal to you a thought that causes negative feelings. Take time to think about it. Remember that emotions are friends and not enemies. Negative emotions show us that there are strongholds fueling the negative feelings. Pray, "Lord, show me my negative thought patterns. Help me see clearly these destructive thoughts in my life."

- Think about a situation that triggered your feeling negative emotions. Write it down at the top of the paper in just one or two sentences. The situation will be the trigger point. Pray, "Lord, show me a recent situation that led me down the path of death instead of life. Show me a time when I began to feel down emotionally, and help me trace it to a specific situation."

- Write down any negative thoughts, emotions, and behaviors. Put them under their respective columns. Ask yourself, *What is behind the thought? What am I really thinking? What am I feeling? How am I behaving?* Pray, "Lord, help me see my negative thoughts, emotions, and behaviors. Reveal them to me today."
- Determine the stronghold by looking for the strongest negative reaction in your thoughts. Look at your "Thoughts" list. Which one gives you the strongest reaction? The strongest thought is usually the main stronghold. Strongholds are usually "I" statements and relate to our identity. The Enemy will always attack your identity in Christ. Pray, "Lord, show me the strongholds in my life. Help me get to the root thought."
- Confess any false beliefs or strongholds in your life to the Lord as sin. We must confess that we have believed these lies instead of God's truth because they are an offense to God. Pray, "Lord, I confess the false belief of [name the stronghold] as sin. I realize that I believe a lie rather than Your truth. I repent. Make me aware of this belief every time I encounter it."

HOW TO HELP OTHERS BREAK PERSONAL STRONGHOLDS. Once you have learned to break your personal strongholds, it's easy to help others break their strongholds. Meet in a quiet place with someone who is struggling against a stronghold. Get a paper and pen, and do the preceding exercise. Have the person think of a situation in which he or she suddenly fell into a negative emotion, such as fear, anger, or depression. The situation can be recent or a long time ago. Write it down at the top of the paper in one or two sentences and make three lists: "Thoughts," "Emotions," and "Behaviors." Have the person give you his or her thoughts, emotions, and behaviors while you fill in the sheet. Find the thought that has the strongest emotional response, as it is usually the stronghold. Have the person repent of the stronghold before God, and then pray for him or her. Together go through the section in this chapter called "Choose Life" and end with "My Prayer to God." This can also be done in a group setting. Remember that breaking strongholds is not a one-time victory. It takes time for new truth to sink in.

MY PRAYER TO GOD

Lord, make me aware of how the Enemy tries to defeat me through strongholds in my mind. I ask for Your divine power to demolish the strongholds in my life. Make me aware of these negative thought patterns. Show me where I have embraced a lie rather than Your truth. Help me study and speak the truth of Your Word. Help me repent quickly when I realize that I have believed a lie. Make me alert to these lies. I bring before You these strongholds, powerful and destructive thoughts, and confess them to You as sin. Wash away my sin and speak Your truth into my heart. I choose to believe Your truth. Today I choose life. I choose Your ways. I choose to obey You and believe Your truth about myself and others. I choose victory over my thought life. In Jesus' name, amen.

CHAPTER NINE

THE INTERCESSOR AND FORGIVENESS

If we confess our sins, he is faithful and just and will forgive us our sins and purify us from all unrighteousness.

— 1 John 1:9

SHE WAS IN her eighties, and as I talked with her, I could sense the deep sadness in her voice and the heavy, unbearable weight she carried. While working at CBN (Christian Broadcasting Network) as a telephone prayer counselor, I received a telephone call from this elderly Christian woman who longed for freedom from the past. CBN gets thousands of calls daily from people struggling with various problems — depression, anger, hurt, drugs, unforgiveness, sin, fear, you name it — and I had the special privilege of talking with this woman. She was downcast and deeply burdened with sin that she had been carrying most of her life. I listened in sadness as she told me her story.

When she was a teenager, she had gotten pregnant. At that time, abortions were illegal, but this woman did not want to keep her baby. By using a sharp object, she gave herself an abortion and managed to live through it, though it greatly damaged her emotional life. When she did marry, she became pregnant two more times, but she did not want to have either child. She aborted the babies. All her life, she carried around the shame and guilt, never having told a single person.

Now she was in her eighties, and the guilt of her sin was too much to endure. She had to tell somebody, to confess her sin, so she called CBN and sadly told me her story, asking for forgiveness for the hidden sin that haunted her. We prayed, and she confessed her sin and repented specifically, asking God for forgiveness. I was able to declare her forgiven, and she was able to receive that forgiveness and cleansing. What a moment that was! She praised God for forgiveness of sin, and she hung up the telephone as perhaps one of the most joyful people in the world. God had washed away her sin, and even though she was elderly, it was as if she were a brand-new person. She walked in a new freedom in her life.

For those who want to grow in intercession, there is a need for a clean heart. We must forgive everyone who has hurt or offended us. We need to know God's forgiveness of our own sin. But how can we forgive others? Can we really receive forgiveness from God and others? Is there a way to walk in freedom? Let's discover the power and freedom of forgiveness and see how we can choose to forgive those who have hurt us.

THE POWER OF FORGIVENESS

We have been sent into the world to implement the rule of God on earth. Where there is discord we are to replace it with harmony. Where there is hatred we are to replace it with agape. Where there is an offense simmering into a murderous conflict, we are to replace it with forgiveness. When we choose to forgive, we invade the realm of darkness and defeat those dark forces with the power of a resurrected life.

— Dudley Hall, "The Toxic Choice"

Forgiveness is one of the most powerful, Christlike responses that we could ever have, yet the steps in forgiving others—or even receiving forgiveness—may be difficult. The love of Christ is the only way we can set free those who have deeply wounded us. The love of Christ gives us the only context we have for believing that God has forgiven us.

There is perhaps no greater gift you can offer God than a heart that knows the power of forgiveness and decides to set others free. Forgiving shows that the love, grace, and mercy of Jesus are operating in our lives. It is time to access this life-changing grace of forgiveness. Is there someone who has offended you? Are you able to release the person in forgiveness? God gives us divine power to forgive. We who have received the freedom of forgiveness have the power to set one another free. This is a power that truly sets the captive free and can affect the whole world. Forgiveness defeats darkness on a massive scale because it involves the resurrection power of Jesus. Nothing can defeat the greatness and glory there is in one act of forgiveness.

The need for forgiveness can be seen in a story of a father and his son in Spain. They had become angry and bitter toward one another. The son finally left home and ran away. His father began to search for him but was unable to find him anywhere. After months of frantically searching, the father came to the end of his resources and sat down sadly in a coffee shop. Suddenly he had an idea! He put an ad in a Madrid newspaper. The ad said something like this: "Dear Paco, meet me in front of the men's clothes shop at 2 p.m. on Friday. You are forgiven. I love you. Your father." On Friday at 2 p.m., eight hundred Pacos showed up! They were all looking for forgiveness and love from their fathers. How important it is that we seek forgiveness and offer forgiveness to one another. It is critical to our lives in every dimension—spiritually, physically, emotionally, and relationally.

Writer Francis Frangipane prompts us with these words:

Would you like to see the Lord shatter the spiritual prisons in your life, the areas where you feel trapped? Then forgive those who put you there, for surely the walls of your imprisonment are made of your own anger and unforgiveness toward others.[1]

Here are some basic steps toward extending and receiving forgiveness:

- **Recognize and call sin what God calls it.** Be specific and thorough. Remember that forgiveness is not excusing and approving of inappropriate behavior or saying that an offense isn't important. Be honest with yourself and recognize your emotional response. You may feel angry, sad, let down, or disappointed. It isn't wrong to have emotions. They are natural. It's what you do with your emotions that can be sinful. Make sure there is no offensive way in you (see Psalm 139:23-24).

- **Share with God honestly and let Him heal you.** Tell God what happened to you and how you feel. Look at His evaluation of the situation. Focus on Him and His faithfulness. Spend time with Him, and let Him restore where sin has destroyed. Forgiveness releases God's divine healing power. Remind yourself, "O LORD my God, I called to you for help and you healed me" (Psalm 30:2).
- **Set the offender free, understanding that it is a process.** Declare forgiveness. Say, "I forgive [name the individual or group] for [name the offense]." Don't say, "I want to forgive." It takes time to go through the process of forgiveness. The hurt can come up at different times, and we must choose to forgive again. It doesn't mean we automatically forget the offense. Paul knew this: "Be kind and compassionate to one another, forgiving each other, just as in Christ God forgave you" (Ephesians 4:32).
- **Release the offender to God.** Repent of your desire to punish or take revenge. Let God deal with the offense. Focus on today rather than the past. Let the offender off the hook. Declare God as judge over the person and the situation, as Paul reminds us to do: "Do not take revenge, my friends, but leave room for God's wrath, for it is written: 'It is mine to avenge; I will repay,' says the Lord" (Romans 12:19).
- **Bless the offender.** Apply God's forgiveness. Trust and reconcile when possible, but realize that forgiveness does not always mean we have to relate to the person in the future. In some cases, this is not possible. Know God's protection and justice. Paul tells us, "Bless those who persecute you; bless and do not curse" (Romans 12:14).

We are God's called-out people, who know who we are in Christ and walk in love with God and one another. We become partakers of His resurrected life. Forgiveness is essential if we want to walk in personal and corporate revival.

God will give us the grace to fully set everyone free. May we be like Jesus, who was the first one to love. When God forgives us, He gives us the power to forgive. May the river of God's life flow through us in that we bless everyone we meet. May we remind people of how much they are loved by God. As we give our lives away in love and forgiveness, we become free ourselves.

Bear with each other and forgive whatever grievances you may have against one another. Forgive as the Lord forgave you.

— Colossians 3:13

THE CHOICE OF FORGIVENESS

Forgiveness is not a spiritual gift, a skill, or an inherited trait. Forgiveness is a choice. Jesus looked down on those who had ruthlessly and mockingly nailed Him to a cross, yet He cried out: "Father, forgive them, for they do not know what they do" (Luke 23:34). How, then, can we refuse to forgive those who have committed offenses against us?

— Henry and Richard Blackaby, *Experiencing God, Day-by-Day*

Some time ago while in Germany, I had the privilege of teaching a session on forgiveness as a part of a training course for individuals serving God in many nations. The course was called Face to Face and was about coming face-to-face with God in intimacy. In order to do this, we must learn to walk in forgiveness. Forgiving those who have hurt us is a personal choice, but sometimes the hardest choice is to forgive ourselves — or to accept God's forgiveness of us. Truly forgiving can be very difficult for our flesh; however, it is one of the greatest ways we can reflect the reality of our walk with God.

Unforgiveness keeps us from God and hinders our prayer life. Living in forgiveness is key for each of us who want to grow in prayer and intercession. We naturally want to blame others and take revenge. Choosing to forgive is an act of the will against human nature.

We see forgiveness demonstrated in the life of Joseph in the book of Genesis. He is a tremendous example of choosing to forgive family members who had deeply hurt him. Through Joseph's act of forgiveness, God used him to bring about a great deliverance in the lives of his family. Joseph had every reason to be bitter. He lived in prison for years because his brothers had sold him into slavery. When he rose to a position of power in a strange land, he could have lorded it over his unknowing brothers and exacted the ultimate in revenge. However, he chose to forgive and be reconciled to his family. He had no bitterness or sense of revenge when he forgave them. He was so full of forgiveness that he begged his brothers to forgive themselves: "Do not be distressed and do not be angry with yourselves for selling me here, because it was to save lives that God sent me ahead of you. . . . But God sent me ahead of you to preserve for you a remnant on earth and to save your lives by a great deliverance" (Genesis 45:5,7). Joseph saw how God used the past, even though painful, for His highest glory and his family's greatest good.

We all know that forgiveness can be difficult to extend or receive. Just as Joseph had to forgive his brothers, today there are many examples of difficult situations that need the incredible grace of God in order to choose forgiveness. But it can be done, and it can bring tremendous blessing. This will especially speak to the unsaved among us.

Let me tell you about a recent amazing story of forgiveness. One German Bible translator, one Turkish pastor, and another Turkish believer were murdered in Turkey because of their Christian faith. It was sudden and unexpected. Turkey enjoys freedom of religion, and these men were a light in that country, simply trying to love the Turks. A few days after their deaths, two of their wives publicly forgave their husbands' killers. They told people that they could forgive because Jesus had forgiven them and He wanted them to forgive their enemies. It was an act that stunned the community and attracted national attention. These women made a choice to forgive in an incredibly difficult situation. I believe that their demonstration of forgiveness will be a testimony that touches the world. Nothing shows the power of God like forgiveness. You and I can make the same choice on a daily basis.

Henry and Richard Blackaby remind us,

There is nothing so deeply imbedded in your heart that God's grace cannot reach down and remove it. No area in your life is so painful that God's grace cannot bring total healing. No offense committed against you is so heinous that God's love cannot enable you to forgive.[2]

Let's beware of the following hindrances that can keep us from choosing to forgive:

- **Lack of understanding of God's judgment and righteousness.** We think we must take the matter into our own hands. If we don't think others are being punished properly, we try to help God. We must trust Him to be judge and get out of the middle of things.
- **Pride in our lives.** We want to be right. We don't think others deserve forgiveness. We may think that there is no need to forgive. We forget that we, ourselves, have already experienced the rich, undeserved forgiveness of God through Jesus' sacrifice. Now we are called to extend that grace toward others.
- **An unwillingness to face the pain of the offense.** We must know that we can bring the pain of any offense to Jesus. Jesus bore all sin: "He was pierced for our transgressions, he was crushed for our iniquities; the punishment that brought us peace was upon him, and by his wounds we are healed" (Isaiah 53:5).
- **Bitterness in our hearts.** We may hold revenge and want to punish. Bitterness and unforgiveness bind us to the offender. We must cut the rope and be set free.
- **Not regarding sin seriously enough.** Sin is serious business. We cannot rationalize nor try to explain away a sinful response on our part. Unforgiveness puts a barrier between the Lord and us.

We need God's help to forgive. Jesus knows the pain of betrayal. He understands humiliation, misunderstanding, shame, and hurt. Jesus is the greatest example of one who forgave others freely and fully. Our Father God develops and shows His character in and through us by allowing us to experience difficult situations, His grace enabling us to react in a Christlike way that gives Him honor. The choice to forgive opens the prison doors so that we are able to walk in a new freedom. As a result, we can walk in righteousness, peace, and joy, demonstrating the life of Jesus here on earth.

The choice to forgive opens my own prison doors. When I choose to hold someone in my debtor's prison, I am the captive. My mind is occupied with justifying why they are there. I become obsessed with their punishment being carried out. In choosing to become their judge, I become their jailer and ironically enough, their captive.
— Dudley Hall, "The Toxic Choice"

THE FREEDOM OF FORGIVENESS

Search me, O God, and know my heart; test me and know my anxious thoughts. See if there is any offensive way in me, and lead me in the way everlasting.
— Psalm 139:23-24

Seeking forgiveness from God and others is the way to walk in wholeness and freedom. The weight of sin is very heavy. A famous psychiatrist, Karl Menninger, once said that if he could convince the patients in psychiatric hospitals that their sins were forgiven, 75 percent of them would be well enough to leave the next day! Why does anyone want to carry such a burden, imprisoned and wearied by the weight of personal guilt?

An example is in the life of David (see 2 Samuel 11). He had sinned by sleeping with another man's wife. After discovering that Bathsheba was pregnant, he sent her husband, Uriah, to the front lines of battle and then withdrew the supporting troops. Sure enough, Uriah was killed in battle and Bathsheba became David's wife. But David felt the weight of his sin. He finally repented and cried out for joy, peace, and a clean spirit before the Lord. He said in Psalm 51:12, "Restore to me the joy of your salvation and grant me a willing spirit, to sustain me." When he repented, God set him free and gave him a pure heart, a steadfast spirit, and new joy.

You may be tired of carrying a heavy burden of sin. We find joy and freedom when we make a decision to repent of our transgressions before God and others. We need to ask God to show us the secret places in our hearts where we may be holding resentment against someone. We need to be aware of how much we need forgiveness ourselves. Here are some practical steps you can take toward forgiveness:

- **Accept full responsibility where you have sinned.** Don't blame-shift; own your part. Should you ask for forgiveness and not receive it from another person, God hears and will free you.
- **Be aware of pride or self-pity in your life.** Pride thinks there is no need to forgive, and self-pity thinks that others don't deserve forgiveness. Understand the cross of Christ and what that really means. God has forgiven you, and He gives grace to the humble.
- **Admit you're wrong.** Say, "What I said was wrong." Don't

minimize your responsibility when you have sinned by saying, "If I hurt you." You must fully admit your sin.

- **Ask for forgiveness.** When you ask, be sure to name the sin. "Please forgive me for [name the sin]."
- **Seek reconciliation when it is possible.** "First go and be reconciled to your brother; then come and offer your gift" (Matthew 5:24).

If we want to grow in intercession, we must walk in holiness and purity. It is absolutely necessary that there is no sin blocking our relationship to God, for anyone who wants to come to God must have clean hands and a pure heart. Learning to repent quickly when we fall is key to a successful prayer life. I once heard that you could tell how mature a Christian was by the distance of time it took between sinning and asking God for forgiveness. Walking in daily holiness and confessing all known sin must be one of our greatest ambitions. It is one of our greatest weapons in intercession.

Forgiveness is the very spirit of heaven removing the hiding places of demonic activity from the caverns of the human soul. It is every wrong made right and every evil made void. The power released in forgiveness is actually a mighty weapon in the war to save our cities.

— Francis Frangipane, "Forgiveness and the Future of Your City"

PERSONAL
APPLICATION

HOW TO SEEK FORGIVENESS FROM OTHERS. This exercise is designed to search your heart in your relationship with others. If you would rather seek forgiveness from God or go through the steps in forgiving others, you may do that instead. Start by reading aloud 1 John 1:8-9. With pen and paper in hand, examine your heart silently before the Lord. Write down any names of people with whom you have a broken relationship. Write down any specific situations relating to these people. Then prayerfully go through the following steps in seeking forgiveness from others:

- Seek reconciliation when it is possible. Remember Jesus' instruction to "go and be reconciled to your brother; then come and offer your gift" (Matthew 5:24).
- Take full responsibility for your sin. Don't shift the blame. Own your part 100 percent.
- Be aware of pride or self-pity in your life. Understand the cross of Christ and what that really means. God has forgiven you, and He gives grace to the humble.
- Admit you're wrong. Don't minimize your offense. Say, "What I said [or did] was wrong."
- Ask for forgiveness. When you ask, be sure to name the sin. "Please forgive me for [name the sin]."

HOW TO HELP OTHERS SEEK FORGIVENESS. Get together with another person or group to pray together for God to search your hearts. Read 1 John 1:8-9, and then spend time going through this assignment individually before the Lord, writing down your personal sins and names of people with whom you have a broken relationship. If possible, have a cross, made out of wood or cardboard, in front so individuals can bring their sins to the cross. I have seen this done with a big wooden cross on which people actually nail their sin papers to the cross, and then the sins are removed, put in a pile, and burned in front of everyone. But you can think of a creative way to demonstrate that our sins are nailed to the cross. In conclusion, have a time of prayer, praising God for forgiving us.

MY PRAYER TO GOD

Lord, You are the greatest example of forgiving others freely and fully. Help me take full responsibility for my actions and admit sin in my life. Don't let me hide or justify it. Show me any area in which I have fallen short. Lord, I receive Your forgiveness and cleansing [see 1 John 1:9]. I praise and worship You for forgiveness in Jesus. If I have sinned against someone, help me admit my wrong and ask for forgiveness. Help me seek reconciliation [see Matthew 5:23-24]. I want to be one who builds unity with others. Help me to be like Joseph, who was able to forgive those who had deeply hurt him. Take all bitterness out of my heart. I thank You for the power of forgiveness, and I choose to forgive everyone who has hurt me. Help me set [name anyone who has offended you] free and release them to You [see Romans 12:19].

Help me bless those who have hurt me [see Romans 12:14]. Help me walk in righteousness, peace, and joy, demonstrating Your life here on earth. I choose to be kind and compassionate, forgiving others, just as You forgave me [see Ephesians 4:32]. In Jesus' name, amen.

CHAPTER TEN

THE INTERCESSOR AND REVIVAL

Oh, that you would rend the heavens and come down, that the mountains would tremble before you! As when fire sets twigs ablaze and causes water to boil, come down to make your name known to your enemies and cause the nations to quake before you!
— Isaiah 64:1-2

IT WAS ONLY a taste, but it made me hungry for more.

We were at sea in the Pacific Ocean on our way to New Zealand. The problem was, the thirty-foot-high swells were too high for our little ship as it bobbed up and down in the ocean. We were anchored outside of Auckland, unable to go into port. We simply had to sit out at sea until the weather changed. But even this delay was all in the perfect plan of God.

Nerves had been on edge, and some of the men had been bickering significantly. Leaders were secretly praying for God to break through in that department. Because of the disputes in the deck department, one of them gave a public apology to the crew. It was our regular Thursday night prayer meeting, and God had something special in mind.

The young man hesitantly faced the ship's crew. He confessed his sin and sat down. But something unexpected happened. Suddenly another person got up and made an open confession of wrongdoing. Then one after another, crewmates began to repent of personal sin. Soon God was putting His finger on everyone's sin. Confessions went on into the early morning hours.

The next day was our normal Friday morning devotions together as the ship's crew. Still anchored at sea, we had expectant hearts, not knowing exactly what would happen. But God was in charge, and the confessions began and continued for several hours, just as they had the day before. The next day, the same thing happened until finally the entire ship's crew, over three hundred of us, made a corporate recommitment of our lives to God.

Sure enough, after the time of rededication, the ocean waves stopped and we were able to enter Auckland as forgiven, refreshed individuals. It was a taste of the beginning of revival; I will never forget that time. It's made me want more, realizing that there is so much more that God wants to give us.

You may be thinking, *What are the characteristics of revival? How can I prepare for something like this?* Let's look at the characteristics, both human and divine, and the ways that we personally can get ready for revival.

THE HUMAN CHARACTERISTICS OF REVIVAL

All the true revivals have been born in prayer. When God's people become so concerned about the state of religion that they lie on their faces day and night in earnest supplication, the blessing will be sure to fall.

— E. M. Bounds, *E. M. Bounds on Prayer*[1]

Many of us pray that God will send a revival among us. We intercede not only for ourselves but also for those around us, asking God to move in powerful new ways. But what does revival actually look like, and how should we pray?

My husband and I had the wonderful privilege of living in Wales for more than a year. A great revival swept through the land in 1904, making an impact on the nation—and the world—in a short span of time. We had the added blessing of visiting Moriah Chapel, the tiny church building where the Welsh Revival broke forth. I was amazed at how insignificant in appearance the building is. Yet the power of God spread around the world from that humble place. Believers in Wales are praying for another mighty revival to touch their land, and we have been inspired to think, study, and pray much for revival since that time. The topic of revival brings great interest to most of us because we long for God to sweep through our country. But we must realize that it is costly, and each of us must be willing to pay the price to prepare for it.

Behind the concept of revival is the Hebrew word *chayah*, which means "to live." In Strong's Concordance, the word is translated "make alive, nourish up, preserve, quicken, recover, repair, restore, save, keep alive and make whole."[2] Who among us does not desire that the church be quickened, made whole, preserved, and kept alive? We must pray with heartfelt passion for this to happen. And it will. When the church is revived, she will be stronger and mightier against the powers of darkness. She will be a brighter light in this dark world. She will be victorious and attract the lost.

When revival hit Wales, the whole community was shaken by the power of God. Crowds would go to the prayer meetings at 6:00 a.m. Because the Holy Spirit affected many people, the entire community was soon turned into a praying multitude. Evan Roberts, the young man God greatly used in the Welsh Revival, would speak of four tenets or keys to walking in revival. These are helpful as we seek personal and corporate revival in our own lives:

1. The past must be made clear by sin being confessed to God and every wrong to man put right.
2. Every doubtful thing in the life must be put away.
3. There must be prompt obedience to the Holy Spirit.
4. There must be public confession of Christ.[3]

We live in serious times. We need to cry out fervently to God, asking Him to revive His church worldwide. We need to be in intensive prayer, asking God to move in our cities and nations. Studying the characteristics of revival will help us prepare both personally and corporately for a great move of God in His church. Understanding the deep need to prepare our own hearts for revival and learning how to cooperate with God as He pours into the earth will keep us from hindering the move of God as it comes.

The key phrase of the Welsh Revival in 1904 was, "Bend the church and save the world." Let's look at the main human characteristics of revival:

Spiritual Preparation. Unity and prayer are two key elements needed for revival. We must pay this price of spiritual preparation. Revival will not come without a hunger and thirst for God that brings intense prayer. There must be a longing to see Him manifest and for His glory. We cannot be indifferent or apathetic but must rend our hearts with the cries that are born by the yearnings in God's heart.

Forty days after Jesus ascended to heaven, His followers obediently prepared for spiritual revival: "They all joined together constantly in prayer" (Acts 1:14).

Conviction of Sin. In true revival, people are seized by an overwhelming conviction of sin. Even the smallest sin seems big. Sin is not taken lightly, and God deals with both the saved and the lost. Revival is intensely personal; God convicts you of personal sin, and your soul is in the agonizing grip of a holy God. Often there is weeping because of the awful conviction of sin. In one revival, the hearers were holding themselves up against the sides of the pews because they felt as if they were sliding into the pit.

The writer of Acts tells us about that first revival crowd, "They were cut to the heart" (Acts 2:37).

God-Consciousness. In revival, there is a consciousness of God, an awareness of His holiness and power. People caught up in revival know without a doubt that God is there. They feel a divine magnetism toward His presence. Evangelist Winkie Pratney reminds us, "There was nothing humanly speaking, to account for what happened. Quite suddenly, upon one and another came an overwhelming sense of the reality and awfulness of His Presence and of eternal things. Life, death and eternity seemed suddenly laid bare."[4]

On the day of Pentecost, "everyone was filled with awe" (Acts 2:43).

May God prepare each of us to pay the price for revival — the price of fervent prayer and allowing Him to work deeply in our lives. Let us ask Him to make us conscious of His presence and learn to abide in Him moment by moment. Pray that He will convict us of even the smallest sin in our lives. Press on in prayer and fasting for revival in the nations. A worldwide end-times revival is going to be a glorious thing, but it will be costly.

We lived on a book exhibition ship for years. In some countries, thousands of visitors came on board daily. Long hours of hard work consumed our full attention. Are we ready for the demands of revival? God must prepare us, His church, personally and corporately for the self-sacrifice that revival entails. May we not draw back but prepare to lay hold of this glorious end-time outpouring of God with all our hearts as the radiant bride of Christ who is willing to sacrifice all so that people might be saved.

Will you not revive us again, that your people may rejoice in you? Show us your unfailing love, O Lord, and grant us your salvation.
— Psalm 85:6-7

THE SUPERNATURAL FIRE OF REVIVAL

In a Sunday morning prayer meeting for these young people the pastor asked for testimonies of spiritual experiences. . . . At last a young girl named Florrie Evans, who had been gloriously converted a few days before, stood and with a trembling voice said: "I love Jesus Christ — with all my heart!" With these simple words the sparks that God had planted in so many hearts burst into flame and the great Welsh Revival began. The fire spread quickly.
— Rick Joyner, "The Welsh Revival"[5]

Revival spreads like fire. It moves supernaturally and spontaneously with a divine drawing that is beyond human understanding. A testimony of love from a new believer sparked the Welsh

Revival that touched the world. God spread the fires of revival unexpectedly. Every revival involves the preparedness of people and the supernatural sovereign hand of God. The Welsh Revival displayed a deep conviction of sin and an awareness of the holiness and power of God. Humans prepare in earnest prayer and soul-searching conviction. Then God comes in a sovereign and supernatural way, spontaneously and with neither striving nor human control. Let's look at the way God works supernaturally in revival.

Spontaneous and Unexpected Working. The Welsh Revival came dramatically in November 1904 on the exact day in both the north and the south of the country. There were no special organizations, meetings, or preaching involved when the Welsh Revival started. It started suddenly and spontaneously.

Luke described the sudden revival that swept Jerusalem on the day of Pentecost: "And suddenly there came" (Acts 2:2, NASB).

Supernatural Manifestations. God can do in a moment what human strivings can never achieve. It is God's divine supernatural work and not man's. In one revival in 1859, there were sudden, supernatural, and extraordinary manifestations. Pratney describes for us, "They were still taken by surprise, so sudden, so powerful and extraordinary were the manifestations of the Spirit's Presence. . . . About one thousand people were suddenly, sensibly and powerfully impressed and awakened."[6]

Luke reminds us of the origin of the Pentecost revival: "There came from heaven" (Acts 2:2, NASB).

Divine Drawing. There is a divine consciousness in revival, a divine drawing from God. Winkie Pratney again helps us understand this process:

As one man was praying, all present became aware that the prayer was heard and that the Spirit of God was being poured out on the village. They left their house to discover the villagers also were leaving their cottages and making their way, as though drawn by some unseen force, to one point in the village. There they assembled and waited. When Duncan Campbell commenced to preach, the word took immediate effect. In a few days, the small community had been swept by the Spirit of God and many souls truly converted.[7]

Luke reminds us that what began in a private gathering soon captured the attention of a city: "When they heard this sound, a crowd came together in bewilderment" (Acts 2:6).

Will your testimony of love toward Jesus and your fervent prayer spark the end-times revival? Or will it be all of us together testifying to our love for God and earnestly praying in unity that will prepare the way for God to spread the supernatural flame that will touch the world?

On an unexpectedly cold day, I had to start a fire in our wood-stove to keep warm. The big logs wouldn't catch fire, but it was the tiny twigs broken together that seemed to catch hold of the match's flame. Quickly the fire blazed. Let us each realize that we must be broken, united in prayer, and bent on God's glory alone to be prepared for the release of the fire of God and His supernatural workings. May God personally touch each of us so that we might be the twigs broken together in prayer before Him. Let us do our part, and our Sovereign God will do His in His own timing and way.

Revival is divine intervention in the normal course of spiritual things. It is God reveal-ing Himself to man in awful holiness and irresistible power. It is such a manifest working of God that human personalities are overshadowed, and human programs aban-doned. It is man retiring into the background because God has taken the field. It is the Lord making bare His holy arm and working in extraordinary power on saint and sinner.
— Winkie Pratney, "The Nature of Revival"

PREPARATION FOR REVIVAL

Prepare the way for the Lord, make straight paths for him. Every valley shall be filled in, every mountain and hill made low. The crooked roads shall become straight, the rough ways smooth. And all mankind will see God's salvation.
— Luke 3:4-6

We are right now living in desperate days. The church in many parts of the world needs revival, and God wants to use each one of us to prepare the way for His moving. It is truly time to cry out to the Lord. The valleys of defeat must be filled, the mountains of disbelief must be leveled, the crooked places of dishonesty must be straightened, and the rough places of disobedience must be made smooth. Almost twenty-five years ago, I wrote in my personal newsletter the following paragraph, and I find that today I must still ask myself the same questions.

> "Am I desperate enough for revival?" "Do I realize the des-perate condition of my country?" And if I trust in religious organization, material wealth, popular preaching, shallow

evangelistic crusades, there will never be revival. But when confidence in my flesh is smashed and I realize my desperate wretchedness and emptiness before God, then and only then will God break through. "Lord, make me ready for revival. Revive me." I challenge you to join me in prayer for revival for our lives and for the nations. I call for prayer that is strong, prevailing, and believing and that takes all that we are and have. God Himself will motivate us to pray these prayers that have extraordinary consequences if we are only willing, willing to pay the price. Pray that God may fill us all with the very passion of Christ and with the power and persistence of the Holy Spirit.

How do we personally prepare for revival? Andrew Murray encourages us:

The coming revival must begin with a great prayer revival. It is in the closet, with the door shut, that the sound of abundant revival will be first heard. An increase in the secret prayer of ministers and members will be the sure herald of blessing.[8]

Prepare Yourself in the Way of Blessing Through Intensive Prayer. Pray with all your heart, asking God to enlarge your prayer and worship life. Make time for God, and practice fasting. Remember God's words, "If my people, who are called by my name, will humble themselves and pray . . ." (2 Chronicles 7:14).

Be Serious About Personal Revival. Instead of watching TV, pray. Don't get caught up in the ways of the world. Lay aside those worldly pursuits. The rest of 2 Chronicles 7:14 reads, "and seek my face and turn from their wicked ways, then will I hear from heaven and will forgive their sin and will heal their land."

Become Dissatisfied with Sin, and Ask God to Convict Your Heart. Be sensitive to His conviction.

> *Search me, O God, and know my heart;*
> *   test me and know my anxious thoughts.*
> *See if there is any offensive way in me,*
> *   and lead me in the way everlasting. (Psalm 139:23-24)*

Revival begins with us. It is all of us individually getting our lives straight and turning from the crooked paths. Just as we experienced personal conviction on our ship when we were bobbing up and down outside of New Zealand, God is dealing with His church. Take seriously the need for personal revival. Take seriously the need for prayer.

The great work of intercession is needed for this returning to the Lord. It is here that the coming revival must find its strength. Let us begin as individuals to plead with God, confessing whatever we see of sin or hindrance in ourselves or others. If there were no other sin, surely the lack of prayer is matter enough for repentance, confession, and returning to the Lord.

— Andrew Murray, *Andrew Murray on Prayer*

PERSONAL APPLICATION

HOW TO PERSONALLY PREPARE FOR REVIVAL. Take time to be still before God. Get a notebook and pen and write down whatever thoughts come to mind regarding the characteristics of revival and preparing for revival. Begin by reading the Sermon on the Mount in Matthew 5–7. Pray for God to speak to you personally as you apply the following points in your life.

- Repent thoroughly. Don't tolerate sin in your own life. Let godly sorrow over your sin touch you deeply. Heed the psalmist:

  > *Against you, you only, have I sinned*
  >   *and done what is evil in your sight. . . .*
  > *Surely you desire truth in the inner parts;*
  >   *you teach me wisdom in the inmost place.*
  > *(Psalm 51:4,6)*

- Make restitution whenever possible. Make sure that your relationships are right: "Live in harmony with one another" (Romans 12:16).
- Practice living the Sermon on the Mount. Matthew 5–7 is the best description of holy living. Ask God to transform your life and teach you to live to please Him: "Blessed

are the poor in spirit, for theirs is the kingdom of heaven. Blessed are those who mourn, for they will be comforted" (Matthew 5:3-4).

- Choose to narrow your interests. If you narrow your interests, God will enlarge your heart. We can so easily be distracted in life, but revival calls for a focused vision on what really matters. "I seek you with all my heart; do not let me stray from your commands" (Psalm 119:10).
- Make a new commitment to reach out to the lost. Ask God for opportunities, and He will help you. Share Christ with those who do not know Him. Follow the example of Jesus. "The Son of Man came to seek and to save what was lost" (Luke 19:10).
- Develop your faith in God. Begin to expect God to move. Believe that God does want to pour out His spirit and bring revival. "Faith is being sure of what we hope for and certain of what we do not see" (Hebrews 11:1).
- End with "My Prayer to God" (found at the end of this application).

Read through this list regularly, letting God speak to your heart.

HOW TO HELP OTHERS PREPARE FOR REVIVAL. Get with an individual or group, pray together, and read the Sermon on the Mount in Matthew 5–7. Have each person respond in a notebook to the above points. After about thirty minutes or when everyone is ready, come together for a time of sharing. End with a season of prayer, asking God to revive your lives. Include the preceding list of directives in your prayers. Close with "My Prayer to God."

Lord, bring revival into my life. I choose to confess my sin and make every wrong right in my relationships. I choose to remove every doubtful thing in my life and promptly obey Your Spirit. Help me to be Your living witness and to walk in unity with other believers. Show me any relationship where I need to make restitution. Help me live in harmony with others [see Romans 12:16]. Convict me of sin in my life. Make me aware of Your holiness and power. Help me to pay the price of revival in earnest prayer. Help me to practice living the Sermon on the Mount. Prepare me spiritually, and work deeply in my life. Make me dissatisfied with sin and desperate for revival. Awaken Your church, Lord, and let it start with me. In Jesus' name, amen.

CHAPTER ELEVEN

THE INTERCESSOR AND THE WORLD

You are the light of the world. A city on a hill cannot be hidden. Neither do people light a lamp and put it under a bowl. Instead they put it on its stand, and it gives light to everyone in the house. In the same way, let your light shine before men, that they may see your good deeds and praise your Father in heaven.

— Matthew 5:14-16

THE MEAL WAS quite delicious. It was a Moroccan dish called couscous. The rice was piled high with all kinds of tasty surprises inside: chicken, vegetables, potatoes, and spices. We eagerly ate with our fingers Moroccan-style as the maid shyly served us.

A group of us were visiting some friends in Morocco. After this typical act of hospitality—a wonderful, unhurried meal enjoyed together in the company of friends—the men went out to watch a group of young people play soccer while the women visited with our host. During that time, I noticed the Muslim maid who spoke little or no English as she took our dishes away to the kitchen. I could tell by her expression that she was troubled. Through the translation of our host family, we finally asked her if we could pray for her. She immediately nodded her head.

We then gathered around her and began to pray one after another. We prayed fervent heartfelt prayers in English as she stood in the center of our little circle. Tears came to her eyes, and she began to weep. God had touched her deeply in spite of the language barrier. The Holy Spirit ministered to her heart in a way that touched all of us. We don't know what God did in her life that day, but we certainly know that He did something special.

While in North Africa, I realized that reaching that region of the world for God was going to take an army of dedicated prayer warriors and a passionate, loving bride of Christ to dismantle the ruling powers of darkness that now captivate and imprison millions of people. What will speak to the multitudes? It has to be people who are completely captivated by God Himself, who are dedicated to His heart for the world and filled with His love and compassion. This will move the hearts of the people because they really are looking for His true love and compassion to fill the God-sized void in their lives.

It is you and I, as we are increasingly in love with God and His cause, who will make the difference. You may ask, *How can I bring the touch of Jesus into my world through my personal prayers? How can my personal prayers change the world?* Let's look into the heart of God for the nations and discover how we can be the salt of the earth and the light of the world through our prayers and lifestyle.

BRINGING THE TOUCH OF JESUS THROUGH PRAYER

What a marvelous thing it is that Christ uses us, His body, to introduce His power to heal into the fabric of everyday life. Whether in a phone call, a chance meeting on the street, in our homes and work places, or within the church walls, bringing the touch of Jesus to others, one prayer at a time, is a profound privilege and wondrous joy for every believer.

— Tricia McCary Rhodes, "Changing Lives One Prayer at a Time"

Each of us needs the personal touch of Jesus that we receive through prayer. Personal prayer is a powerful way to effectively help one another. A single prayer uttered by the anointing and direction of the Holy Spirit can actually change the course of people's lives. Let us, therefore, be ever ready to pray for others. In traveling to different nations, praying for and with many people for their burdens and concerns, I'm convinced that personal prayer brings victory to the lives of others and carries great eternal reward. Let us neither forget nor neglect this simple ministry by which the Lord changes lives from distress to joy.

The touch of Jesus through prayer has no limitations. Once, my husband and I were walking in France when a man collapsed on the ground nearby. His granddaughter was on her bike crying. People began to gather, and the man, hardly moving, was helpless with his face in the dirt. Not knowing the language, we tried to find out what had happened but with no success. We finally bent down, put our hands on his body, and began to pray. After a few minutes, he sat up. An ambulance soon came, and by that time, he was able to talk, and they took him away.

I believe that our simple prayer made a difference at that moment. Jesus is our example: "When the men of that place recognized Jesus, they sent word to all the surrounding country. People brought all their sick to him and begged him to let the sick just touch the edge of his cloak, and all who touched him were healed"

(Matthew 14:35-36). His touch brought healing, and our prayers can do the same.

Do we realize the power of God that extends to others as we bring the touch of Jesus into individual lives through prayer? Personal prayer is a key in life, both in the areas of giving and receiving it. We all have occasions when we feel the Enemy's attack or are going through a low period. What a joy to receive personal prayer! It is like a breath of fresh air to a gasping soul. It may lead us on a new path. While encouraging our hearts, it can change the directions of our thoughts.

On the *Doulos*, a man named Gary prayed regularly for more than three hundred people on board. He still has a list of all their names, asks for prayer requests, and often tells them he is praying while he inquires as to their welfare. In this ministry, he is faithfully bringing the touch of Jesus to them. Think of how pleased you would be to serve with a person like Gary. He is making a difference.

Terry Teykl, author of "Ushering People into God's Presence," says,

Simply put, personal prayer ministry is one person ushering another into God's presence through prayer. It is a human encounter through which God ministers to the needs of one of His children. It is grace in action, and it can happen at any time, in any place.[1]

How can we, too, bring the touch of Jesus into the lives of those we encounter in our everyday lives?

- **Be aware of the needy world around you.** Enter each day with a desire to minister the life of Jesus to others in some way. Ask the Lord, "To whom can I minister today? Make me aware of the needs of others, and show me for whom You want me to pray." Watch for God to open doors of opportunity. Have an expectant heart. Believe that God wants to use you every day in some way to bless others with the touch of Jesus. The Holy Spirit will guide and give you opportunities.

- **Ask God for guidance, and learn to listen and wait.** Wait upon God for guidance. Listen to the Holy Spirit. He will guide you in prayer that will reach deeply into the spirit of others. Learning to wait before praying helps in praying the prayers God desires rather than ones we think are important.

- **Go forth in faith, and ask individuals if you can pray for them.** Many times people are afraid to offer prayer because they think that lost people don't want prayer. Actually the opposite is true. People are more willing for us to pray for them than we realize. When we go out willingly to pray for others, God sees our faith. These little steps of faith are like seeds that will bring forth a large harvest in due season. My husband and I train others in prayer evangelism by encouraging them to pray for the needs their neighbors express. Try it, and I believe you will be surprised at the response.

- **Realize that spiritual need is at the core of the problem.** Many times physical and emotional problems are connected to the spiritual realm. Be sure to pray through possible areas of sin and any strategies of the Devil. Often someone comes to me with a surface problem and I find a spiritual stronghold at the core. Though we may start with the mention of a surface problem, as we pray, God reveals the spiritual stronghold so we can bring it before the cross. We then find that the surface need is met.

- **If God reveals a course of action, encourage the person to follow through.** It may be confession of sin, restitution toward others, or some act of obedience. Encourage the person to obey the Lord and to follow through by taking action.

- **Stop when you are done.** Sometimes we try to help the Holy Spirit, but He may want the person to approach Him alone. Faith grows the most when people take action themselves. We need to know when we are finished so we don't hinder the progress of others by doing everything for them.

- **Keep your motives pure, making sure God gets the glory.** We want God to be glorified. Continually give Him praise and thanksgiving after ministering in prayer to others, knowing that it was all His work and we were His privileged vessels.

Bringing the touch of Jesus to others through prayer is a great joy. My husband and I regularly go the 24/7 House of Prayer located in our city, a place designated for prayer at any time, day or night. A ministry for the whole city rather than an individual congregation, it enhances the corporate prayer within a city and helps to bring the atmosphere of God into the city. Recently, on three different occasions, individuals came into the prayer room to spend time with God. Three times we were able to pray for their personal needs. A couple came with a desperate marriage and had been separated for three months. We prayed for them, asking God to restore their marriage, and He did. A man came who was sick and had six epileptic seizures in one day. We prayed for his healing and that the seizures would stop. He hasn't had one since. A woman came who needed a job and had no money. We prayed for a new job and gave her some money. She was greatly encouraged.

In each of these situations, we experienced God's grace in action. We experienced His authority and power as we ushered these individuals into the presence of God through prayer. We can learn to minister like Jesus not only for individuals but for whole nations as well.

As we learn to minister like Jesus, we will listen more and talk less, wait longer, and make fewer proclamations. When we can see what the Father is up to, we find a new authority and power in personal prayer ministry.

— Tricia McCary Rhodes, "Changing Lives One Prayer at a Time"[2]

LOOKING INTO THE HEART OF GOD FOR THE NATIONS

Nothing was more pressing than that the nations and multitudes who are marching to a Christless eternity should be saved. How I saw the agendas of men: so many and varied and all of such vital importance to them, but there was only one paramount agenda to God: The nations. . . . All else was rather trivial in comparison and we all had majored on the trivial.

— Michael Howard, *Tales of an African Intercessor*

While at sea for days on a ministry trip in the vast, seemingly limitless ocean, it was easy to feel low—especially if seasickness struck. I found it was a prime opportunity to seek to see things from God's point of view. Undistracted by the business of usual routines, I was able to look at God's world, taking time to hear His heart of love for the nations. His heart is full of compassion and is big enough not only to care for the individual but also to care for the whole world as well. What does this mean to us as intercessors and as people who want to grow in prayer? We looked at how we can bring the personal touch of Jesus as we pray for individuals, but our focus should also include the world—the nations and cities around us. We are the ones who can impact countries with our prayers.

God is looking across this whole earth to find those whose hearts are as His, those who will intercede. Will you be one to stand in the gap? God is looking for intercessors. Will you be one who intercedes for the nations? Will you let God lay a country on your heart for the purpose of prayer? Can God give you His passion for the world? A key to our authority is when our heartbeat aligns with the heartbeat of our almighty God.

While a student at Moody Bible Institute, I was impacted by the life of school founder Dwight L. Moody. He was known for his effectiveness in winning souls to Christ. During one of his famous evangelistic tours, several British clergymen asked why he could be so effective. He was just an uneducated man. He then brought them to his hotel room. Pointing out the window, he asked them what they saw. Each man described the people below. Moody looked out the window with tears streaming down his cheeks. He told them that he saw thousands of souls that will spend eternity in hell if they do not find Christ. Moody saw people differently from the average person. He saw eternal souls, and it changed his whole approach to life. We as intercessors must see the lost just as he did. This will impact not only our prayer lives but the way we live as well.

Begin to pray for the world. Ask God to lay a burden on your heart for a nation, a people group, or a particular region. You may want to pray for troubled areas of the world you hear about in the news. God wants every one of us to open our eyes, enlarge our vision, and begin to pray for the needy world around us. There are many ways to pray. Some intercessors like to pray through prayer cards with prayer requests for different nations. Others like to pray over a large map of a country. Some like to use the book or website for Operation World, which lists detailed requests for every nation.[3] Each method is valuable, but the main thing is to begin.

As you incorporate prayer for the world into your prayer life, be creative. Let the Holy Spirit lead you. Let Him burden your heart for different parts of the world. Adding countries into your prayer life develops your effectiveness in a powerful way. I like to pray for a different nation every day. Your burden for the world will grow, and you will begin to see the world and life in a new way. Our own problems seem smaller when we focus on the needs of whole countries and people groups. Bringing the touch of Jesus to the nations is a powerful way to pray.

The following are excellent prayer requests when interceding for any nation. Don't think you have to pray through the whole list, but let God direct you by His Spirit. Pray the scriptural truth over the nation as well.

- **Thank God for how He is working in the nations.** "How awesome is the LORD Most High, the great King over all the earth! . . . God reigns over the nations; God is seated on his holy throne" (Psalm 47:2,8).
- **Pray for just laws, for righteous moral standards, and that the Word of God will be given its rightful place.** "Righteousness exalts a nation, but sin is a disgrace to any people" (Proverbs 14:34).
- **Pray that God's people will walk in holiness, the fear of the Lord, and obedience.** "Since we have these promises, dear friends, let us purify ourselves from everything that contaminates body and spirit, perfecting holiness out of reverence for God" (2 Corinthians 7:1).
- **Pray that the church will reach out to the poor, needy, and imprisoned.** "Remember those in prison as if you were their fellow prisoners, and those who are mistreated as if you yourselves were suffering" (Hebrews 13:3).
- **Pray for God to send His workers into the harvest field.** "Go and make disciples of all nations, baptizing them in the name of the Father and of the Son and of the Holy Spirit, and teaching them to obey everything I have commanded you. And surely I am with you always, to the very end of the age" (Matthew 28:19-20).
- **Pray that 24/7 prayer and worship will start in every major city in every nation.** "These I will bring to my holy mountain and give them joy in my house of prayer. Their burnt offerings and sacrifices will be accepted on my altar; for my house will be called a house of prayer for all nations" (Isaiah 56:7).

Praying this way may be one of the most strategic things you will ever do. One day we will worship God around the throne in heaven with people from every tribe and tongue and nation. We will then realize the value of every prayer we prayed for a nation while we were on the earth. Are you willing today to pray for the world? Are you willing to invest your time in a task so rewarding? Catch hold of the atmosphere of heaven when it comes to the heart of God for the lost. He died for the whole world.

And they sang a new song:

"You are worthy to take the scroll
   and to open its seals,
because you were slain,
   and with your blood you purchased men for God
   from every tribe and language and people and nation."
(Revelation 5:9)

While I am very excited about what is happening, yet as an intercessor, I can never forget that over half of the world's population has never heard of Jesus. The task ahead is still enormous. As darkness covers the earth in the last days and darkens the people, the glory of the Lord will shine brighter and brighter, brighter and brighter in the face of a people who love Him absolutely and uncompromisingly. In this way, the whole world will know that there is a God who reigns in the Heavens and man will be left without excuse on the day of Christ's appearing. The Spirit is still heralding a call for watchmen to join the great choir of intercessors.
— Michael Howard, *Tales of an African Intercessor*

THE SALT OF THE EARTH AND THE LIGHT OF THE WORLD

God's people are His preserving agents for a world that is corrupted and degenerating because of sin. Your life is designed and commissioned by God to enhance a community and to preserve what is good and right. There is deep significance today for a godly life that is involved in its community. The presence of Christ in you makes all that He is available to others. His salvation can free an addict, mend a broken home, heal the pain of the past, restore a wayward child, and comfort a grieving heart. All of this is available to those around you as Christ expresses His life through you.

— Henry and Richard Blackaby, *Experiencing God, Day-by-Day*

In the ministry of prayer and intercession, we must remind ourselves daily that we are to be salt and light. It is with a sobering sense of responsibility that we realize that the very life of God in us touches the world around us wherever we are. Just as Jesus, we must not only pray in our closet but also recognize that as we rise from our knees and go forth, we are God's hands, feet, and mouths to a lost and desperate world. We are commissioned to live our daily lives speaking words of life and truth to those who are hurt, broken, and lost. What a tremendous task this is!

Our prayers have tremendous effect on the world, and often God uses us to be the answer to our prayers. We are the ones to reach out and speak the truth of the gospel. Begin to pray for God to give you opportunities to shine His light into the world and enhance what He wants to do in the lives of your friends, coworkers, and neighbors. We must live what we believe. Isaiah 61:1 was the job description of Jesus:

> *The Spirit of the Sovereign LORD is on me,*
> *because the LORD has anointed me*

to preach good news to the poor.
He has sent me to bind up the brokenhearted,
  to proclaim freedom for the captives
  and release from darkness for the prisoners.

This is how He lived His life on earth. Because His Spirit is living in us, we, too, must live and love as Jesus did. He has anointed us for this task.

People all over the world are trusting in the wrong things to save them—good works, false religions, cults, and so on. Others are trying to forget the emptiness in their hearts through such things as drugs, sexual relationships, and drinking. But there is a tragic end to those who are not trusting in the all-sufficient God to save them. Salvation is in Jesus Christ alone. How important it is for us to be God's light in our world through our prayers and through our actions.

HOW TO FIND ETERNAL LIFE

- **GOD LOVES YOU.** "This is love: not that we loved God, but that he loved us and sent his Son as an atoning sacrifice for our sins" (1 John 4:10).
- **YOU HAVE SINNED.** "All have sinned and fall short of the glory of God" (Romans 3:23).
- **THE RESULT OF SIN IS DEATH AND SEPARATION FROM GOD.** "The wages of sin is death, but the gift of God is eternal life in Christ Jesus our Lord" (Romans 6:23).
- **JESUS DIED FOR YOUR SINS.** "God demonstrates his own love for us in this: While we were still sinners, Christ died for us" (Romans 5:8).

- **JESUS IS THE WAY TO ETERNAL LIFE.** "Jesus answered, 'I am the way and the truth and the life. No one comes to the Father except through me'" (John 14:6).
- **HEAVEN IS A FREE GIFT.** It can't be earned or deserved. "It is by grace you have been saved, through faith — and this not from yourselves, it is the gift of God — not by works, so that no one can boast" (Ephesians 2:8-9).
- **RECEIVE JESUS TODAY AS YOUR SAVIOR.** "God so loved the world that he gave his one and only Son, that whoever believes in him shall not perish but have eternal life" (John 3:16).

Admit that you are a sinner and can't get to heaven yourself. Be willing to turn from your sin. Believe that Jesus died for you on the cross. Through prayer, invite Jesus Christ to come into your life.

"Dear Lord Jesus, I know that I am a sinner and need Your forgiveness. I believe that You died for my sins. Forgive me for my sins. I now invite You to come into my heart and life. I want to trust and follow You as the Lord and Savior of my life. Thank You for the free gift of eternal life. In Your name, amen."

We should no longer hide our lights. It's time for every intercessor to step out by faith and shine for Jesus in this dark world. Reaching out with the gospel of Jesus always lights a bigger flame of passion in my own prayer life. Because we are the salt of the earth and lights in the world, with hearts full of thanksgiving to God, we need to pray that the church will fulfill its responsibilities in a world that is dying without Christ. Matthew 5:13-15 says, "You are the salt of the earth. . . . You are the light of the world. A city on a hill cannot be hidden. Neither do people light a lamp and put it under a bowl. Instead they put it on its stand, and it gives light to everyone in the house." Continually radiate the gospel message and the light of God's glory.

I encourage you to realize all that you have in Christ. May the truth presented in this book motivate you in your prayer life. You have the chance to develop intimacy with the living God. You can choose to depend on Him, and this opens the way for His unlimited opportunity to bless you. You can learn to speak words of life that can uplift and bring grace to everyone you meet. You can hear God's voice and walk in the purposes of God for your life. May your personal prayers change the world!

You can learn how to pray the promises of God and cultivate perseverance in prayer even in difficult situations. You can learn to pray God's purposes rather than dwell on your own problems. You have the ability to make God your stronghold and choose life rather than death. You can know what it means to be forgiven for everything you have ever done wrong. You can personally prepare for the revival that is coming on the earth and bring the touch of Jesus to others through prayer. This gives you and me every reason to thank and praise God.

Henry and Richard Blackaby remind us,

There is no mistaking the effect of light upon a darkened place. Light boldly and unabashedly announces its presence and vigorously dispels darkness. God's desire is to fill you with His light. He wants you to shine as a brilliant testimony of His presence and power in your life, so that the darkness in the lives of others around you will be displaced by the light of God's glory.[4]

What practical steps can we take toward filling the world with God's light and changing the world through personal prayer? Thank God that:

- **We are the salt of the earth and give the flavor of Christ to the world.** "You are the salt of the earth. But if the salt loses its saltiness, how can it be made salty again?" (Matthew 5:13). Pray that the church would be salt to the earth.
- **We can preserve a community by our presence.** "The LORD replied, 'My Presence will go with you, and I will give you rest'" (Exodus 33:14). Pray that the church will take the presence of God into the marketplace and neighborhoods. Pray that signs and wonders will follow.
- **The Holy Spirit in us is greater than the demonic forces in the world.** "You, dear children, are from God and have overcome them, because the one who is in you is greater than the one who is in the world" (1 John 4:4). The Holy Spirit through us acts as a barrier, holding back the full force of lawlessness in nations. Pray that the church would realize and appropriate the power of the Holy Spirit.
- **We can overcome evil with good.** "Do not be overcome by evil, but overcome evil with good" (Romans 12:21). Pray that goodness and holiness would be characteristic of the church even in the midst of the darkest of situations.
- **We are God's ambassadors on earth.** We have the authority of heaven and represent heaven's government. "We are therefore Christ's ambassadors, as though God were making his appeal through us. We implore you on

Christ's behalf: Be reconciled to God" (2 Corinthians 5:20). Pray that the church would live as Christ's ambassadors on earth, sharing the good news of salvation.

This chapter may be ending, but the rest of your life is only beginning. Use it for God's glory. You can dispel darkness through your prayers and your life. Praise God for all that we have in Christ and seek to be the salt of the earth and the light of the world everywhere we go.

There was no ignoring Jesus' arrival upon earth! Darkness was dispelled! Everywhere Jesus went, God's truth was boldly proclaimed, people were healed, hypocrisy was exposed, and sinners found forgiveness. The world was never the same once the Father introduced His light through His Son. Can that be said of you as well? Do your co-workers recognize the light that is within you? Does the presence of Christ radiate from your home into your community? When God's light is allowed to shine unhindered through your life, the darkness around you will be dispelled.

— Henry and Richard Blackaby, *Experiencing God, Day-by-Day*

PERSONAL APPLICATION

HOW TO PRAY FOR THE WORLD. Spend an hour praying and praising God for the following as it relates to the world and to your city. Pray for the countries of your choice. Do this every day this week, selecting a different nation each time. Incorporate prayer for the world into your prayer life, combining your prayers with Scripture. End with "My Prayer to God."

- Pray the promises of God in His Word over the nations. Pray Psalm 96 over a nation of your choice: "Declare his glory among the nations, his marvelous deeds among all peoples" (verse 3).
- Pray for unity and revival in the body of Christ. Jesus said, "I in them and you in me. May they be brought to complete unity to let the world know that you sent me and have loved them even as you have loved me" (John 17:23).
- Pray for government leaders and spiritual leaders. Paul exhorts, "I urge, then, first of all, that requests, prayers, intercession and thanksgiving be made for everyone—for kings and all those in authority, that we may live peaceful and quiet lives in all godliness and holiness" (1 Timothy 2:1-2).
- Pray for the salvation of the lost. "Everyone who calls on the name of the Lord will be saved" (Acts 2:21).

- Thank God that we are the light of the world. "You are the light of the world. A city on a hill cannot be hidden" (Matthew 5:14). Pray that the church would not be hidden. Pray that our light would intensify.

HOW TO HELP OTHERS PRAY FOR THE WORLD. Get together with an individual or group and read together Psalm 96. Then begin to pray through this psalm for various nations or a nation that you choose together. Declare God's glory, marvelous deeds, salvation, splendor, and majesty over that nation. Also, using Scripture as your basis, incorporate the preceding prayer requests into your prayers. Let God lead you as you pray. End with praying together "My Prayer to God."

MY PRAYER TO GOD

Lord, help me to bring the touch of Jesus into my world. Make me aware of the needy world around me. Open doors of opportunity in which I can touch another person with Your love. Give me faith and courage to pray for others. Give me a vision for prayer for the world. I want my personal prayers to change my world. Help me to pray for the nations. Lord, I want to be Your salt and light [see Matthew 5:13-16]. Help me to reach out to the lost and needy. I thank You that You have anointed me to preach good news to the poor, to bind up the brokenhearted, and to proclaim freedom for the captives and release from darkness for the prisoners [see Isaiah 61:1]. Enable me to do this in my world. In Jesus' name, amen.

CONCLUSION

Arise, shine, for your light has come, and the glory of the Lord rises upon you. See, darkness covers the earth and thick darkness is over the peoples, but the Lord rises upon you and his glory appears over you.
— Isaiah 60:1-2

THIS IS THE season for intercessors and for all believers to arise and shine the light of the gospel through their lifestyles and prayers wherever they go. While I was writing this book, my heart leapt within me as I sensed the urgency of the hour and the spirit of intercession that is stirring the world, bringing forth the rule of Jesus and His kingdom. I feel an incredible joy as I realize that this is the day for intercessors to arise to their high calling of prayer. Personal prayers will change the world. It is exciting to see intercessors coming forth in the strength of the Lord for the demands of the hour. They are saying yes to the Spirit of God and to the high cost of intercession. They are arising with a greater determination and anointing than ever before. Young and old, male and female, they come to this glorious calling that Jesus is gloriously, lovingly, and powerfully magnified.

My prayer for you is that you not only arise to your own calling in intercession but also lead many into this tremendous ministry of prayer and intercession.

May God help you to lay hold of the truths in this book and apply them to your life.

May your prayers become red-hot in their passionate fervency.

May you walk forth with strength of character and a steadfastness of resolve that is unstoppable by any Enemy attack.

May you know your authority to effectively release God's power across the territory God has assigned to you.

May your love for Jesus grow stronger and stronger with each passing day with your praises ascending to the throne of grace as a fragrant incense filling the heavens with the beauty of your devotion.

Intercessor, it is time to arise and shine. Never forget that the Lord rises upon you and that His glory appears over you for such a time as this. Your calling to intercede is during the finest hour, at the greatest moment in all of history. Truly, you have been called to the kingdom for such a time as this. May your personal prayers change the world around you. May you demonstrate to the world that heaven exists and God is sovereign ruler and does answer the prayers of His people in exceeding greatness and glorious power.

Arise, shine, for your light has come.

NOTES

INTRODUCTION

1. E. M. Bounds, The Necessity of Prayer as found in *E. M. Bounds on Prayer* (New Kensington, PA: Whitaker House, 1997), 212.

CHAPTER ONE: THE INTERCESSOR AND INTIMACY

1. Brother Lawrence, *The Practice of the Presence of God* (Grand Rapids, MI: Revell, 1967), eighth letter.
2. Rick Warren, *The Purpose-Driven Life* (Grand Rapids, MI: Zondervan, 2002), 90.
3. Mike Bickle, "The Bridal Paradigm" (Kansas City, KS: Friends of the Bridegroom, 2002), 116.

CHAPTER TWO: THE INTERCESSOR AND FAITH

1. E. M. Bounds, The Necessity of Prayer as found in *E. M. Bounds on Prayer* (New Kensington, PA: Whitaker House, 1997), 107-108.
2. E. M. Bounds, Purpose in Prayer as found in *E. M. Bounds on Prayer* (New Kensington, PA: Whitaker House, 1997), 110.

3. Bounds, 110.
4. Bounds, 111.
5. Leonard Ravenhill, *Why Revival Tarries* (Eastbourne, UK: Kingsway Publishers, 1999), 38.
6. Bruce Wilkinson, *The Prayer of Jabez* (Sisters, OR: Multnomah, 2000), 44.

CHAPTER THREE: THE INTERCESSOR AND CHARACTER

1. E. M. Bounds, Essentials in Prayer as found in *E. M. Bounds on Prayer* (New Kensington, PA: Whitaker House, 1997), 294.
2. Bounds, 294-295.
3. Henry Blackaby and Richard Blackaby, *Experiencing God, Day-by-Day* (Makati City: Church Strengthening Ministry, 1998), 124.

CHAPTER FOUR: THE INTERCESSOR AND STILLNESS

1. Elisabeth Elliot, *Keep a Quiet Heart* (Ann Arbor, MI: Servant, 1995), 135.

CHAPTER FIVE: THE INTERCESSOR AND THE BIBLE

1. E. M. Bounds, The Necessity of Prayer as found in *E. M. Bounds on Prayer* (New Kensington, PA: Whitaker House, 1997), 175.

CHAPTER SIX: THE INTERCESSOR AND PERSISTENCE

1. E. M. Bounds, The Necessity of Prayer as found in *E. M. Bounds on Prayer* (New Kensington, PA: Whitaker House, 1997), 138.

2. Bounds, Purpose in Prayer as found in *E. M. Bounds on Prayer*, 43.
3. Alice Smith, *Beyond the Veil* (Ventura, CA: Regal, 1997), 38–40.
4. Bounds, Purpose in Prayer as found in *E. M. Bounds on Prayer*, 41.
5. Bounds, The Necessity of Prayer as found in *E. M. Bounds on Prayer*, 140.

CHAPTER SEVEN: THE INTERCESSOR AND PURPOSE

1. Carol Man, The 19th Hole (Long meadow), quoted in *Reader's Digest*.

CHAPTER NINE: THE INTERCESSOR AND FORGIVENESS

1. Francis Frangipane, "Forgiveness and the Future of Your City," www.inchristsimage.org.
2. Henry Blackaby and Richard Blackaby, *Experiencing God, Day-by-Day* (Makati City: Church Strengthening Ministry, 1998), 192.

CHAPTER TEN: THE INTERCESSOR AND REVIVAL

1. E. M. Bounds, Purpose in Prayer as found in *E. M. Bounds on Prayer* (New Kensington, PA: Whitaker House, 1997), 98.
2. James Strong, *Strong's Exhaustive Concordance of the Bible* (Nashville: Regal), 39.
3. Rick Joyner, "The Welsh Revival," *The Morning Star Journal*, vol. 2, no. 4 (1992): 45–46. Used by permission. www .morningstarministries.org.

4. Winkie Pratney, "The Nature of Revival," *The Morning Star Journal*, vol. 4, no. 3 (1994): 15.

5. Rick Joyner, "The Welsh Revival" *The Morning Star Journal*, Vol. 2, No. 4. Used by permission. www. morningstarministries.org.

6. Pratney, 23.

7. Pratney, 19.

8. Andrew Murray, *Andrew Murray on Prayer* (New Kensington, PA: Whitaker House, 1998), 559.

CHAPTER ELEVEN: THE INTERCESSOR AND THE WORLD

1. Terry Teykl, "Ushering People into God's Presence," *Pray!* magazine, May 2004, 22.

2. Tricia McCary Rhodes, "Changing Lives One Prayer at a Time," www.soulatrest.com.

3. www.gmi.org/ow/ offers frequent updates to prayer needs around the world.

4. Henry Blackaby and Richard Blackaby, *Experiencing God, Day-by-Day* (Makati City: Church Strengthening Ministry, 1998), 52.

RECOMMENDED READING

Bickle, Mike. *Passion for Jesus.* Orlando: Creation House, 1993.

Blackaby, Henry, and Richard Blackaby. *Experiencing God, Day-by-Day.* Makati City: Church Strengthening Ministry, 1998.

Bounds, E. M. *E. M. Bounds on Prayer.* New Kensington, PA: Whitaker House, 1997.

Campbell, Wesley, and Stacey Campbell. *Praying the Bible: The Book of Prayers.* Ventura, CA: Regal, 2002.

Campbell, Wesley, and Stacey Campbell. *Praying the Bible: The Pathway to Spirituality.* Kelowna: B.C., Canada, 2003.

Cooke, Graham. *Drawing Close.* Grand Rapids, MI: Chosen Books, 2005.

Damazio, Frank. *Seasons of Intercession.* Portland: BT Publishing, 1998.

Dawson, John. *Taking Our Cities for God.* Lake Mary, FL: Creation House, 1990.

Dawson, Joy. *Intercession: Thrilling and Fulfilling*. Seattle: YWAM Publishing, 1997.

Foster, Richard. *Prayer: Finding the Heart's True Home*. London: Hodder and Stoughton, 1992.

Goll, Jimm. *The Lost Art of Intercession*. Shippensburg, PA: Destiny Image Publishers, 1997.

Greig, Peter, and Dave Roberts. *Red Moon Rising*. Eastbourne, England: Relevant Books, associated with Kingsway Publishers, 2003.

Grubb, Norman. *Rees Howells, Intercessor*. Fort Washington, PA: Christian Literature Crusade, 1962.

Guyon, Madame Jeanne. *Experiencing the Depths of Jesus Christ*. Sargent, GA: The Seed Sowers, 1975.

Haan, Dr. Cornell. *The Lighthouse Movement Handbook*. Sisters, OR: Multnomah, 1999.

Hawthorne, Steve, and Graham Kendrick. *Prayerwalking*. Orlando: Creation House, 1993.

Howard, Michael. *Tales of an African Intercessor*. Kansas City, MO: Out of Africa Publishers, 1998.

Hughey, Rhonda. *Desperate for His Presence*. Minneapolis: Bethany, 2004.

Jacobs, Cindy. *Possessing the Gates of the Enemy: A Manual for Militant Intercession*. Grand Rapids, MI: Chosen Books, 1991.

Johnstone, Patrick. *Operation World*. Waynesboro, GA: Paternoster Publishing, 2001.

Meyer, Joyce. *Battlefield of the Mind*. Tulsa, OK: Harrison, 1995.

Murray, Andrew. *Andrew Murray on Prayer*. New Kensington, PA: Whitaker House, 1998.

Omartian, Stormie. *The Power of a Praying Woman*. Eugene, OR: Harvest House, 2002.

Pierce, Chuck, with John Dickson. *The Worship Warrior*. Ventura, CA: Regal, 2002.

Pray! magazine. Colorado Springs, CO: NavPress, 2007.

Prince, Derek. *Shaping History Through Prayer and Fasting*. New Kensington, PA: Whitaker House, 1973.

Sandford, John Loren. *Healing the Nations: A Call to Global Intercession*. Grand Rapids, MI: Chosen Books, 2000.

Sheets, Dutch. *Intercessory Prayer*. Ventura, CA: Regal, 1996.

Silvoso, Ed. *That None Should Perish*. Ventura, CA: Regal, 1994.

Smith, Alice. *Beyond the Veil*. Ventura, CA: Regal, 1997.

Smith, Eddie, and Alice Smith. *Drawing Closer to God's Heart*. Lake Mary, FL: Charisma House, 2002.

Smith, Eddie, and Alice Smith. *Spiritual Housecleaning*. Ventura, CA: Regal, 2003.

Sorge, Bob. *The Fire of Delayed Answers*. Canandaigua, NY: Oasis House, 1999.

Towns, Elmer L. *Fasting for Spiritual Breakthrough*. Ventura, CA: Regal, 1996.

Tozer, A. W. *Knowledge of the Holy*. San Francisco: Harper and Row, 1961.

Wagner, Peter. *Prayer Shield*. Ventura, CA: Regal, 1992.

Wilkinson, Bruce. *The Prayer of Jabez*. Sisters, OR: Multnomah, 2000.

For a more extensive reading list, see www.intercessorsarise.org.

ABOUT THE AUTHOR

DEBBIE PRZYBYLSKI is the founder and director of Intercessors Arise International, a part of the ministry of the Elijah Company, Inc. The vision of Intercessors Arise International is to see a multitude of intercessors from every nation released in strategic prayer for the furtherance of the gospel worldwide. Debbie's passion is to see intercessors at work stirring the nations and setting captives free throughout the world by the ministry of prayer. She believes that intercessors must be trained, encouraged, and released for the end-times harvest.

Debbie's husband, Norman, is the founder and director of the Elijah Company, Inc. Debbie serves alongside him in their ministry of training, equipping, and mentoring future and active missionaries by identifying, instructing, imparting, and impelling them to God's designated mission field. Some related aspects of training offered by the Przybylskis are seminars and training courses in intercession, missions, power evangelism, breaking free from spiritual strongholds, and the Lighthouse of Prayer ministry.

Debbie served for more than twelve years with Operation Mobilization, ministering to people from all over the world. Her wide range of experience includes evangelistic and motivational speaking, coordinating and teaching people in evangelism, and training others in intercession, 24/7 prayer, and the skills needed for living and relating cross-culturally. She also is available to missionaries and international women who need counseling. Debbie graduated with a diploma in Bible theology and a diploma in Christian education from Moody Bible Institute, and a master's degree in cross-cultural Christian education and a master's degree in missions with a certificate in counseling from Columbia International University. She and Norm have ministered in more than sixty countries.

ABOUT INTERCESSORS ARISE INTERNATIONAL

Conferences, Seminars, and Training Retreats

Norm and Debbie Przybylski travel worldwide teaching, training, and mentoring on various themes related to missions and intercession. Their topics include prayer, intercession, 24/7 prayer, breaking strongholds, power evangelism, world missions, and missionary training. One of their specialties is their Missionary Training Camps, which launch people into their missionary call. For information about hosting an event with Norm and Debbie, contact them at the address at the end of this book.

Books, CDs, and Other Resources

The Przybylskis have produced articles and materials relating to prayer and missions, including an Ekballo Missionary Training Manual and a set of CDs of their Missionary Training Camp. Visit their websites for more information. www.elijahcompany.org or www.intercessorsarise.org.

Intercessors Arise International Website

Intercessors Arise International wants to unite, motivate, train, and network the corporate strength and vision of intercessors worldwide in order to see a release of God's power and glory for the furtherance of world evangelization. The Intercessors Arise International website is designed for this purpose. For more information, go to www.intercessorsarise.org.

International School of Prayer

The Intercessors Arise International website includes an International School of Prayer to train people in intercession and prayer for intercessors in every nation. This school helps beginners as well as seasoned intercessors network with the worldwide prayer movement and learn how to pray strategically for cities and nations worldwide. The International School of Prayer is informative, biblical, and motivational. To become a part of this school, visit www.intercessorsarise.org.

Training Networks

Norm and Debbie provide training and encouragement through their free e-mail networks. Join the hundreds worldwide who already receive the following network training publications:

- **Intercessors Arise International** is a weekly e-mail publication sent worldwide for intercessors and those interested in growing in prayer and intercession. It is designed to train, encourage, motivate, inform, and release individuals and prayer groups in intercession. To subscribe, send a blank e-mail to intercessorsarise-international-subscribe@strategicnetwork.org.

- **Intercessors Arise America** is a weekly e-mail publication for intercessors in America. To subscribe, send a blank e-mail to intercessorsarise-america-subscribe@ strategicnetwork.org.
- **24-7 Prayer Arise** is a monthly e-mail publication for those interested in developing day-and-night prayer and worship for the glory of God, the entreating of His presence regionally, and the furtherance of the gospel worldwide. It is designed to train, encourage, unify, motivate, inform, and release the body of Christ into day-and-night prayer. To subscribe, send a blank e-mail to 24-7prayerarise-subscribe@strategicnetwork.org.
- **Health Arise** is a monthly e-mail publication for those interested in improving their health through nutrition and prayer. To subscribe, send a blank e-mail to health-arise-subscribe@strategicnetwork.org.
- **Intercesores Arriba** is a weekly e-mail publication for Spanish-speaking intercessors interested in growing in prayer and intercession. It is designed to train, motivate, and release individuals and prayer groups in intercession throughout the Spanish-speaking world. To subscribe, send a blank e-mail to intercesores-arriba-subscribe@ strategicnetwork.org.
- **Levantamientoenoracion 24-7** is a monthly e-mail publication for Spanish-speaking individuals and prayer groups who are interested in developing day-and-night prayer and worship for the glory of God throughout the Spanish-speaking world. It is designed to train, encourage, and release the Spanish-speaking body of Christ into

day-and-night prayer. To subscribe, send a blank e-mail to levantamientoenoracion24-7-subscribe@strategicnetwork .org.

- **Elijah Company Mentorship Network** is a bimonthly publication that provides encouragement and instruction for those working in different nations. This publication will help those involved in going to, sending to, praying for, or living in other nations. To subscribe, send a blank e-mail to elijahcompany-mentorshipnetwork-subscribe@ strategicnetwork.org.

For further information regarding Elijah Company, Inc., or Intercessors Arise International, contact:

Elijah Company, Inc.
P. O. Box 64016
Virginia Beach, VA 23467-4016
elijah@elijahcompany.org
www.elijahcompany.org, www.intercessorsarise.org

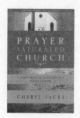

Here's a resource
to help you pray
with more

Power,
Passion,
& Purpose

Every issue of *Pray!* brings you:

- **Special Themes** that deal with specific, often groundbreaking topics of interest that will help you grow in your passion and effectiveness in prayer
- **Features** on important and intriguing aspects of prayer, both personal and corporate
- **Ideas** to stimulate creativity in your prayer life and in the prayer life of your church
- **Empowered**, a special section written by church prayer leaders, for church prayer leaders
- **Prayer News** from around the world, to get you up-to-date with what God is doing through prayer all over the globe
- **Prayer Journeys**, a guest-authored column sharing how God moved him or her closer to Jesus through prayer
- **Intercession Ignited**, providing encouragement, inspiration, and insight for people called to the ministry of intercession
- **Classics**, featuring time-tested writings about prayer from men and women of God through the centuries
- **Inspiring Art** from a publication that has been recognized nationally for its innovative approach to design
- And much, much more!

**No Christian who wants to connect more deeply with God
should be without *Pray!***

Six issues of *Pray!*® are only $21.97*

Canadian and international subscriptions are only $27.97 (Includes Canadian GST).

*plus sales tax where applicable

Subscribe now at www.praymag.com or call **1-800-691-PRAY**
(or 1-515-242-0297) and mention code H7PRBK when you place your order.